Success Story
Hironari Ohshiro

Yes, I've done it, so you can too!

Quenching the Thirst for Global Success
From a tiny island to the world

.

Toshio Maehara

Success Story Hironari Ohshiro
Yes, I've done it, so you can too!
Quenching the Thirst for Global Success
From a tiny island to the world

Copyright: ©Toshio Maehara 2015
ISBN978-0-9861241-0-5

Published by: Maehara & Associates
Printed by: K&M Design Associates

Printed in the United States of America

This book is dedicated to the networkers of the world,
and to all who dream big and live passionately

Foreword

At first glance this book may appear to be a history of the evolution of a successful company, with a unique product and marketing structure. It is however, much more than that.

I was deeply touched by Mr. Toshio Maehara's detailed description of his beloved Okinawa and it's heritage and culture, as well as the strength, honor and perseverance of the people indigenous to it.

The ravages of World War II itself and the post war injustices of the US military, and later the Japanese government could only be overcome by a people strong enough in tradition, courage, and strong family ties and bonds to one another.

Above all, the book is a testament of a deep and

long-lasting friendship between two men based on honor, respect, and trust. Mr. Hironari Ohshiro and Mr. Maehara are of the same age and background, and the author's admiration for his friend comes across as heartfelt and genuine.

The book illustrates the value of persistence, hard work and courage, and the sacrifice necessary to fulfill a dream and prevail against seemingly overwhelming odds.

Enagic is a highly successful company conceived by its founder on a model that strives to improve global health, both physically and economically by underscoring a need for compassion for all beings. With all of his business successes and failures, Mr. Ohshiro has not forgotten his roots, people, or homeland.

He has made the lives of his people in Okinawa better through the sponsorship of schools and opportunities for employment for many with his creative business venture.

I recommend this book to anyone for it's message of hope and encouragement to strive for success with honor and dignity.

The human spirit will prevail when trust, fearlessness, and honor stand against adversity and hopelessness.

Having lost my home and my heritage in WWII

to the Nazis and the Soviet Army, I am touched by its uplifting and hopeful message and inspiration to those who have a dream desire to see it come true

Dr. Horst Filtzer

Preface

Today, more people than ever before are dreaming of success and striving to achieve it. What's more, today more people than ever before have access to the chances and opportunities that will enable them to grasp hold of success. The world has grown smaller; we can now witness the success stories of those around us.

But look closely at the trajectory of a successful person, and you will likely see how, in most cases, these people have travelled a path fraught with great difficulty, adversity, obstacles, failures, and setbacks. Success, it seems, cannot be achieved without failure.

So to those people who dream of success but have yet to achieve it, I say this: perhaps you have simply failed to follow your dream to the end. You have bailed out too soon.

Success is still within research, but to get there, you need energy in order to fuel the tenacity and tolerance you'll need to keep hanging on—just a little longer—until you have reached your goal.

Hironari Ohshiro, the man this book takes as its subject, is a classic example of how to preserve on the path to success. He has overcome challenges, stood firm in the face of setbacks, and always sought to turn adversity into opportunity. His ability to use turn-around thinking and keep a positive attitude has driven him forward. His is a unique success story, for a number of reasons.

Firstly, he managed to create, from nothing, over 650,000 customers for his product around the world in a very short time. Secondly, he has refused to buckle in the face of failure. Thirdly, he has developed a quite distinctive way of doing things. And finally, he embodies the true entrepreneurial spirit, facing up to challenges armed with nothing but determination and imagination.

In the first part of this book, we will trace back to the Okinawan islands of the 1950s, in order to take a glimpse at Ohshiro's roots: his life as a child and the circumstances of the islands where he grew up.

In Chapter 1, we will begin to seek out the

background to his success: the challenges faced, the setbacks overcome, the foundations upon which his business was built. He went from being a young boy on a tiny island to a formidable businessman with a global reputation, quenching his thirst for success as his business expanded throughout world.

In Chapter 2, we turn the focus on Ohshiro himself, by trying to identify aspects of his personality within the company he runs, eventually revealing how his business is, in fact, a projection of him as a unique individual.

In Chapter 3, we will examine what I have termed "Ohshiro-ism", his creative approach to business strategy. Of course, there are some secrets that he is not willing to share. But there are valuable lessons to be learned in what he calls the "science of setbacks". And what becomes clear is how he displays an unwavering entrepreneurial approach no matter what he is facing.

In the final chapter we will look at Ohshiro's work, both within and beyond the company walls, as well as his plans for the future. The chapter also provides a brief introduction to the world of network marketing, also known as multilevel marketing. This information should be useful to people with no experience of network marketing.

This biography was never intended to be a simple

attempt to paint a picture of Hironari Ohshiro, the man. It was conceived in order to seek out the secrets of Ohshiro's success and to provide inspiration and support to the many of us who are still working our way along the path to our dreams. I hope that my readers will discover within themselves the ability to emulate the qualities that have long since led Ohshiro to success.

As Ohshiro himself often says, "Yes, I've done it, so you can too!"

We must also not forget the contribution of his childhood sweetheart and wife, Yaeko, who has been a constant, serene presence throughout his life, by his side and behind his success.

I have tried to cover each episode in the book concisely, to allow the reader to read the book a little at a time, picking it up during a break from work, perhaps, flicking through at the hotel or the airport lobby.

To end, I would like express my gratitude to Dr. Horst Filtzer for agreeing to write the foreword to this book. Dr. Filtzer is a graduate of Harvard University and a cardiovascular consultant; I am truly thankful that he could find the time to write a few words for me. I would also like to thank my editor, Makoto Konoumi, at Word of Life Press Ministries. And finally, I would thank my wife, Mutsuko, for her

14

support in taking notes for me and ensuring that the writing of this book went as smoothly as it could.

I also extend my gratitude to all the other people who have shared their wisdom with me as I wrote this book.

A portion of the proceeds of this book will be donated to the Enagic Golf Academy and to other non-profit organisations.

Toshio Maehara
Rachno Palos Verdes, California
April 2015

Table of Contents

Foreword
Preface

Introduction

Chapter One: Quenching the Thirst for
           Global Success,
           From a Tiny Island to the World

Chapter Two: A Character-driven Company

Chapter Three: Creative Business Sense, Creative Business Strategy

Chapter Four: From Now, The Future

Introduction

Okinawa Back Then

Okinawa, back when? The Okinawa of 50 to 60 years ago, the Okinawa of the 1950s and 1960s. Back when the islands of Okinawa, some 400 miles from the southern coast of mainland Japan, were still desperately poor. Back when the prefecture was struggling with a complex web of problems. Okinawans of my age are all survivors of this period of poverty and of difficulty. Some of us buckled in the face of the struggle, while for others it was the very struggle that drove them to strive for success. Some of us lost our way among this tangle of difficulties, while for others it was this very complexity that allowed them to unravel the knots and find the right path. For some people, being poor is the catalyst they need to strive for success. Others are happy if they can manage to keep things as they already are. People are free to decide which path to take in life, and to follow that path whatever it might be. And being born poor is nothing to be ashamed of; there is no correlation between poverty and immorality. In the same way that being wealthy is no indication of greatness.

Faced with a high mountain, there will be some who long to climb it. Others will fear the height and walk around the mountain. Still others will choose to avoid it, despite being quite capable of conquering the peak. The person I will introduce in this book is someone who will seek to climb any mountain before him, no matter how high it soars. And even if he does not quite reach the top, he will not give up. He will try again, over and over.

All of us have the same roots. None of us were born without a father and a mother. Our roots are important. It is from these roots that the plant grows, forming shoots, spreading out stalks, stretching them into branches. It is on these branches that fruit ripens and the blossoms open. But roots alone are not enough to grow fruit. It is a sad truth that many plants and flowers will wither before they ever bear fruit.

The love of a mother towards her child is of utmost importance, as the tale "Mother Meng's Three Moves" from ancient China tells us; Mother Meng, mother of the Chinese philosopher Mencius, moved her household twice in order to ensure her son was brought up in the best possible environment, only settling once she had found a home next to a school. Mothers look ahead to their children's futures, using different objects and different methods to teach their children about what is important in life. Ohshiro's mother taught him much about how showing compassion to others would mean that, one day, others would show compassion to him. Okinawans—we call ourselves *Uchinanchu*—are often described as being friendly and compassionate. Perhaps these are characteristics shared by many people from Okinawa. Some people who are forced to walk a difficult path will naturally wish for companions on that road. Others will keep their troubles to themselves, seeking only happiness for others. Perhaps it is the case that the spirit of the *Uchinanchu* places the greatest weight on showing compassion to others.

This book is about a man who, when faced with a mountain, has only demonstrated an iron will to climb it. He is powered by that particular brand of compassion unique to Okinawa, a compassion that now allows him to travel around the world without stopping. And he and I can only look upon Okinawa as it is today with amazement, as we compare it to the Okinawa we knew, back then.

Okinawa, Island of Tragedy

At the end of the Second World War, Japan surrendered to the Allied Forces. One of the main conditions of its surrender saw Okinawa placed under the control of a United States Military Government and, subsequently, a United States Civil Administration, thereby breaking it off from mainland Japan. Despite being Japanese, the Okinawan islanders were now under the control of the very people who had so long been their enemies. Perhaps it was the islands' destiny to be separated, in administration as well as distance, from the mainland.

Okinawa saw much sacrifice during the war: over 240,000 deaths, soldier and civilian both, during the Allied invasion of the islands. Of those, around 100,000 were civilians, ordinary Uchinanchu. A total that speaks volumes of the cruelty of the conflict in Okinawa. Why did so many civilians have to die? Who should be blamed for such bloodshed?

Ohshiro is one of six siblings; one of his older brothers died of illness, and his other older brother and one of his younger sisters both died in the war. Ohshiro only just managed to scrape through the conflict with his life. His older sister, Hisako Kawabata, and his younger sister, Kinuko, still live happily in Okinawa to this day, close to where they all grew up. The Second World War was a tragedy: for Okinawa and for the Ohshiros. The main island of Okinawa was left devastated, its lands charred and barren. There was no hope for regeneration, no industry, no commerce. People were left struggling to live hand-to-mouth, destined to walk a path of hardship. The only land battles during the Second World War to take place on Japanese soil were fought on the islands of Okinawa. The islanders, those who experienced the pain and distress of those battles, still bear the mental scars inflicted during the conflict today, seventy years later. Even if the new generation were able to see those scars, they could surely never imagine the unbearable pain that accompanied them.

In 1972, the post-war occupation was brought to a close and the islands of Okinawa reverted to Japanese rule. It immediately became clear that there was a significant gap in living standards between the Japanese mainland and the islands of Okinawa. That gap remains to an extent today, although the "new" Okinawa is now the subject of increasingly intense attention from South East Asia. Perhaps we are about to see Okinawa become the fashionable place to travel. Okinawa is often compared to the Hawaiian economy, and indeed it is the case that Okinawa is becoming increasingly prosperous thanks to the tourism industry and the military industry.

Still, it is my hope that soon, Okinawa will no longer have to rely on a military-based strategy for economic growth. Instead, it will be able to develop and launch Okinawan products, services, and intellectual property which can be showcased to Asia and to the rest of the world and become the new core of Okinawa economic progress.

Cornerstone of Peace: the Soul of Okinawa

In the Second World War, the United States dispatched more than 300,000 troops to fight in Okinawa. At the time, the population of Okinawa was just under 800,000, so it is easy to imagine how utterly outnumbered the islanders were.

Footage from the time shows waves upon wave of American soldiers pouring onto Okinawan beaches. There was no way that the gathered Japanese forces could put up any sort of fight. Junior high school students were conscripted. They were armed with nothing more than bamboo spears, which they were taught how to jab and thrust at approaching US soldiers. It was farcical. On August 15, 1945, the Emperor of Japan announced the country's unconditional surrender.

Surrender meant more sacrifice for Okinawa. US soldiers wreaked havoc, the military government did as it pleased. Responsibility for the bloody battles of Okinawa was placed on the already strained shoulders of the islanders. The island was forced to accept all of the contradictions, the injustice, the inequality. The discrimination and distortion and stress. The island also had to accept all of the war babies abandoned by their American soldier fathers.

Despite the humiliation, the islanders rallied themselves. They never forgot that Okinawa is made up of islands of unique song, of matchless dance. Paradise islands with the power to calm and to heal. In 1995, the islands commemorated the fiftieth anniversary of the end of the battles which so ravaged them. They did so by building a memorial park, in the city on the southernmost tip of the main island of Okinawa. Within the park there is a monument, the Cornerstone of Peace. The monument commemorates everyone who died in the Battle of Okinawa, friend or foe. The American soldiers, the European soldiers, the Japanese soldiers, the citizens of Okinawa. All of their names are inscribed on the monument. Is there any other monument such as this, which commemorates the names of everyone who died, regardless of their nationality or affiliation?

In July 2000, the Japanese government hosted the G8 summit. Bill Clinton, the President of the United States at the time, visited the Cornerstone of Peace, and made a statement in remembrance of those who lost their lives and the legacy of Okinawa as islands of peace. Okinawa is becoming an increasingly popular holiday destination for tourists across Asia, and I hope that the prefecture will become known as an oasis of peace and of calm, superseding its past as islands of war.

We *Uchinanchu* must not be bound by our terrible past. We must move towards new and better possibilities. The Cornerstone of Peace has become a treasure which Okinawa should be proud to share with the world.

A dozen or so years ago, a particular song became popular in Okinawa. It is called *A Prayer for Peace*. The song is a call for peace from a collection of islands which has suffered great tragedy. The lyrics go something like this:

1. Beautiful Okinawa, always a battlefield
   When will we be able to live in peace?
   This island, our island
   Praying for peace for our Okinawa
2. Let none of us forget, this world of pitiful battle
   Burned into the hearts of all of us
   Refrain
3. All of us together, hearts and mind together
   The true Okinawa, for us to protect forever
   Refrain

An International City

Once Okinawa reverted to Japanese rule, the government of Japan invested heavily in making infrastructural improvements to the islands. This injection of finance kick started the regional economy, immediately bettering the lives of the Uchinanchu. Improvement was seen everywhere: roads, communications, education, economy, living standards. But some basic problems remained unaddressed.

At one time, more than half of the main island of Okinawa was sequestered for use by the US military. Today, more than 40 years after the reversion to Japanese rule, the issue of US military presence remains. It's a concern that is intimately linked to the lives of the native Uchinanchu and to the politics of the islands.

Leaving that question aside, let us look at Okinawa today. Naha City in particular has evolved into an international city. There is a constant stream of tourists from the Japanese mainland, from Taiwan, South Korea, Southeast Asia; everyone comes to play and to shop. Naha airport has been transformed from a tiny air strip to an international travel hub. More than 6,000,000 people visit the islands every year; the government of Okinawa is hoping to hit the ten million mark very soon. With a total residential population of 1.42 million, the flow of visitors means that there are around 2 million people on the islands at any one time. To the west, the shores are lined with resort hotels and foreign-owned hotel chains; everything is ready and waiting for an influx of island tourism. The regional tourist board has grand ambitions for Okinawa to be the next Hawaii. But it's not there yet.

Still, Okinawa has oceans of unparalleled beauty. Prefectural trade and commerce is booming, creating a market more than able to meet the needs of new generations of Okinawans.

Any Uchinanchu who has experienced the islands during or immediately after the war must surely be struck by the absolute change Okinawa has undergone. In Japan there is a famous legend, Urashima Taro. He is taken by a turtle to an undersea kingdom for just three days, but returns to find himself hundreds of years in the future, in a world he does not recognize. An Okinawan visiting the island after thirty or forty years can surely sympathize with Taro's feelings in a familiar yet unfamiliar world.

50 or 60 years ago, we were children. We could not have predicted what Okinawa would become. If you are busy thinking about how to survive today, you have no energy left over to think about what might

happen tomorrow. Children were still going to school shoeless. The bags on their back were made at home then stuffed with pencils, notebooks, school supplies. Or at least, something resembling school supplies. School buildings had thatched roofs. Or curved tin roofs, surplus to American army requirements. Tin roofs were hot in summer, cold in winter. The sound of tropical squalls hammering on the tin roof was almost musical. Days without leaks were to be thankful for. Many school buildings had thatched roofs, with straw sacks spread out on simple dirt floors to sit on.

They might sound like something out of a history book, but these are the stories (schools) Ohshiro would have known, too.

360 Yen to the Dollar!

Occupied Okinawa used something called "B yen" as currency, a sort of military scrip. After a time, this was replaced by US dollars. It was all a political gimmick. At the beginning of the 1970s, Japan was rocked by two consecutive shocks. The first was the so-called "Nixon shock", which saw the US open diplomatic relations with China, and the beginning of Kissinger's "ping-pong" diplomacy. The fixed exchange rate changed to a variable rate. Then came the oil shock, which forced Japan to branch out into international diplomacy and international economics. Conservatism was no longer an option. The waves of the global economy began to break against the shores of Japan. Japan had become one of the world's biggest economic powers. One dollar had been worth 360 yen, but that quickly fell: to 300 yen, to 250 yen, to 200, to 100, even down to 70 for a time. The yen soared, but so did the dedication of the European and American markets to products that were "made in Japan".

Back when one dollar was 360 yen, the US troops in Okinawa were able to live it large. They lived in special zones for foreign residents, with home electronics and telephones, shops and school buses. They lived in greater luxury than the native Okinawans could ever imagine. An American missionary working in the US could earn a monthly salary of $800-1000, while Okinawans who had graduated high school or university would be looking at a maximum of $30-50. An American missionary I got to know, who had been dispatched to Okinawa, told me he was earning around $250-300 a month, which gives a sense of what their standing of living must have been like.

Missionaries didn't get paid much, but it was enough to cover housing, insurance, and to save a little for the future. Ordinary Japanese were paid around ¥15,000 monthly. The exchange rate between the yen and the dollar is now three times more in favor of the yen than it had been in the first half of the century. The lifestyles of the US soldiers took an about face.

Occupied Islanders

The occupying US forces discriminated against the islanders: politically, economically, racially. America was conqueror of the world during that time, wielding its power across the globe. Okinawan children would yell "Yankees go home" whenever they saw the soldiers, without really understanding what it meant.

The Uchinanchu were suffering from double discrimination: from mainland Japan and from the occupying forces. Were the islanders destined to be ruled by outsiders? US army and navy personnel left a trail of sexual assaults, nighttime disturbances, violent daytime incidents. It became common for the military presence to disrupt the peace of everyday life. But incidents of sexual assault and murder, allegedly perpetrated by US soldiers, were dealt with by US military courts, with the accused often being found not guilty after a review of unilaterally gathered evidence.

The Okinawans had no jurisdiction. They could negotiate with the Japanese government, but the only response to demands for soldiers to be handed over to the local authorities was the dispatch of those soldiers back to US soil, from where they could not be extradited. No-one ever wants to be the loser in war. The Japanese government was powerless in the face of such unjust justice. Losing the war forced the losers into a state of semi-slavery. History is always written by the winners. For half a century, the relationship between the US and Japan was one of "master and servant". Over time, it shifted to "big brother" and "kid brother".

It was a period which somehow created an environment in which it was all too easy to become servile. People were robbed of their volition; children were robbed of their enthusiasm. Some people gave up. Yet others were different: they felt compelled to live their lives with greater passion than ever. Some people are as stubborn as weeds, fighting on regardless. Others are suffocated by those same weeds, gasping for air before quietly expiring.

Are Okinawans Really Americans?

The people living in Occupied Okinawa were of uncertain status: were they Japanese or American? They needed a passport, issued by the occupying US administration, in order to travel to mainland Japan. At the time, a left-wing political organization was active in Okinawa, demanding the return of Okinawa to Japan. They did not call Japan "Japan", however; they called it hondo, "the mainland", as if Okinawa was an integral part of Japan.

At the time, political activity, and labor movements in particular, were kept under strict control. Members of socialist parties and communist parties were seen as dangerous. The US civilian government treated the activities of community party leaders as political crimes, a good excuse to throw them into prison. The US was forced to monitor any political links between Okinawans and "the mainland". The American strategy was to isolate the islands. Many arguments were raised against the idea of returning Okinawa to Japan: it should be given independence as the Ryukyu Islands; it should be returned to the governance of mainland China; it should become a US territory, much like Guam. For the US, Okinawa was and remains today the key which opened up the whole of the Pacific. For China, the islands were a rich source of oil, much like the still-disputed Senkaku islands. The same political movements from 40 or 50 years ago still resonate today.

The Old Home in Mount Yambaru

Back then, almost none of Okinawa's roads were

paved. The only paved roads were the ones used by the occupying US forces; their tanks and trucks whipped up clouds of sand as they rushed along the roads. The state of the roads was appalling; driving for a couple of hours would leave you with a face ashen with dust. The most common type of automobile was a roofless three-wheeler, and this was how most people travelled between Naha, the capital, and the surrounding regions. There were buses but they were very inconvenient; the waits were long and buses infrequent, sometimes only running every second day. If you missed the bus you were planning on catching, that was it for the day. The buses were also extremely crowded. As for telephones, they were a luxury that only the very rich had in their homes; certainly not something that ordinary people could ever dream of owning. Back then, you couldn't tap out a message on a handheld device and send it wherever you wanted in the world. You couldn't even have imagined such a thing. Progress in telecommunications has truly been revolutionary.

It took a good few hours to drive from Naha to Nago, where Ohshiro was born, in those days. Route No. 1, the critical road that connected the south of the island to the north, is unrecognizable today. It used to take the best part of the day to get to Nago, but now you can set off from Naha on National Highway No.

58 and be there in a blink of an eye. There's barely enough time for a nap. Back then, drivers had to be particularly careful of the nanamagai, a road on the approach to Nago with seven consecutive sharp twists and turns, but today the road has been reconstructed. But it was beautiful, cutting into Nago harbor like the jagged teeth of a saw. Treacherous as it was, I miss it.

The drive would take you through Nago town, with the brewery where Orion Beer—the islanders' favorite—was made on your right, then up east along a lush mountain road, before arriving at the east coast. There were no houses along the way. Once on the coastal road, if you headed north and you would see, off to the right, a US army base, where construction was always ongoing. Today, this sort of destruction of the natural environment is an issue of major concern to the Okinawan government. Ohshiro's home lay inside the coastal road. It was a small rural house, part of a village called Setake. This tiny hamlet today enjoys relative prosperity by growing turmeric. The Kanucha Resort, which today lies just beyond the village, has had a positive effect on Setake since opening. The Enagic Golf Course,

completed just two years ago, will also be a boost to the village. After all, it is now less than two hours from Naha.

Setake is where you can find the elementary school Ohshiro attended. His wife, Yaeko, was also born here. This is where his roots begin.

Setake is and always has been Ohshiro's starting point. Yaeko's family home is a stone's throw from where the Ohshiros lived. You could make it from one house to the other without directions. Perhaps the two of them began to walk in the same direction from their earliest days in the village. Some of Ohshiro's relatives still live in the village today. Ohshiro's first job was in the village office, too. Setake was his whole life, from birth until boyhood.

Their old elementary school is no longer in use today, and the village children now attend a nearby school, formed by the merger of a number of local schools. Ohshiro has rented the old school building, using and managing the building and keeping it well maintained. Doubtless it is because of the affection he feels towards his old school; nevertheless it is strange to see how he is turning back time.

Eventually, Ohshiro would leave his village in Mount Yambaru and make his way to Naha, then Tokyo, then Los Angeles, then further onward to cities all across the world, introducing Kangen Water®, the idea of ionized water, wherever he went. On the way, his entrepreneurial spirit and his determination to quench his thirst for global success, would be tested. But he would struggle onward through the storm, pushing forward towards expansion and success. Ohshiro was to face much drama in the years ahead, but the backstage to that drama would always be the tiny village where his roots begin.

A Man with Three Lives

Ohshiro often talks about how he has "died three deaths". He caught malaria, was hit by a military truck, and later was slaughtered in the video business wars.

The battles left Okinawa with another unwanted and toxic souvenir: malaria. Ohshiro's older brother and younger sister both caught what were thought to be mild cases of malaria, but both died long before Ohshiro, whose illness had been thought more severe. They are considered victims of the war, and their names are carved into the Cornerstone of Peace in memorial park in southern Okinawa. Those who died of malaria were considered blameless victims of the war, no different to those who died more violently. Ohshiro was gravely ill and thought certain to die, but he somehow managed to pull through, despite poor quality of medical treatment. Malaria has a long incubation period; the disease does not manifest itself for a considerable time after infection. Ohshiro's illness was a long one, and his mother had resigned herself to seeing her son die before her. Ohshiro, too, had accepted the inevitable. But death did not befall him. He was a man of providence.

When Ohshiro was twenty two and working in the village office, he suffered a terrible accident. As he turned from a side road onto the main village road, he was hit, face-on, by a large US military truck. He woke, in great confusion, to find himself in a hospital bed. Eventually, the painkillers wore off and he remembered the truck smashing into him. A faint scar from the accident remains slightly visible on his forehead to this day. In those days, when the scars of the war were still raw, military trucks often tore along the narrow village streets. After all, the needs of the US military took precedent over everything and anything else. Ohshiro should have looked both ways, but either way his life had been saved miraculously for a second time. He had survived being hit by a truck and malaria. Is there anything as irresponsible as war?

One of the requirements for success is good fortune—or luck. The temptation is to assume that good fortune is quite outside one's own control. Personally, I think that the things which come into our lives are more than simple coincidence.

So Ohshiro managed to survive two near-deaths. His third near-death experience is detailed in the episode on *Losing the Video Tape Wars*, coming later in the book.

Lessons of Poverty, Lessons from Mother

Ohshiro's family was poor, like most others at the time. They were self-sufficient, growing what they could on a small farm. They had nothing to trade for money. It was a hand-to-mouth existence, each day a struggle to get to the next. There was no hope of saving for the future. Ohshiro was one of six children; he had two older brothers, one older sister, and two younger sisters. His father's health was poor, meaning that his mother had to raise the children virtually alone. They did not enjoy three meals a day; they would be lucky to eat once. The children had to learn to go hungry from a very early age. Illness has always meant finding money to pay for insurance and healthcare. But illness was something that people in poverty just had to learn to live with. These early experiences drilled into Ohshiro the importance—the value—of being in good health.

Ohshiro always talks of his mother with great respect. Despite the difficulties she faced, his mother never gave up, no matter how great the struggle or how abject the poverty. In his later years, recalling how determined his mother was would point Ohshiro in the right direction on his path to success. Poverty is inconvenient, it robs you of opportunity. But it was Ohshiro's mother, with her warmth and affection, who enabled him and his siblings to forget about their poverty. His mother taught Ohshiro how to be considerate and compassionate to those around him, despite his poverty. She also taught him, through example, the importance of not limiting himself.

Enagic's corporate motto is "communicating kindness". The compassion of his mother seems to overlap here with the corporate compassion seen at Enagic. Many of the corporate social actions launched by Ohshiro, some of which will be introduced later, are indicative of just how deeply he was influenced by his mother.

Ohshiro's family home is in a secluded mountain location. It is tiny—seemingly no bigger than the average American garage. But it was here, in this tiny, noisy home, filled with six children, that Ohshiro grew up. I have visited to India and Bangladesh and have seen entire families living in a single room. Ten or more children might be packed into each tiny dwelling. When I saw Ohshiro's home in front of me once again, it reminded me of nothing more than the cramped homes I saw in India. Nobody lives in the Ohshiro family home now, but a large photograph of Ohshiro's mother still hangs on an inside wall, and great care is taken to keep it the way it used to be out of respect for her. The outside walls of the house are painted in pale blue, the Enagic brand color. This is where Enagic was born; whether consciously or subconsciously, it is here where the past and the present intersect.

Ohshiro sees this humble home as both the starting point of his own history and the starting point for the globalization of Enagic. He even keeps this home as his official address, despite owning homes in Tokyo and Los Angeles. For it was from this tiny structure that Ohshiro crawled, then toddled, then walked towards the challenges of life which lay ahead.

From the Country to the Academy

Ohshiro left his village for Naha, the capital. He had happily been offered a place at Naha Commercial High School. There was only one such school on the whole island, which meant fierce competition for places. The school was particularly popular with high achieving students from rural areas. This was their chance to breathe the air of the city for once, and to prepare themselves for better futures. Since it was a

Commercial High School, the students were taught the basics of business, accounting and bookkeeping. There were no calculators back then, so they learnt advanced calculation techniques on the abacus. Some students complained that it was a slow process to see any practical application to their education; they were displeased by the strong academic focus??. At the time, Ohshiro could never have known just what a fundamental contribution to his future this course would make. No opportunity to learn should ever be missed.

The life of poverty he had experienced at home was replaced by a new life, that of a high school student working part-time to make ends meet. Today, many high school students have part-time jobs, but back then it was an indication of the impoverished background of the student. Ohshiro lodged with the relative of one of his high school teachers, and started the hard slog towards financial independence. He was blessed with excellent teachers, who spurred on his desire to learn and to improve himself. One of those teachers, Ryomei Hirayama, showed particular kindness. He stayed with Hirayama for a time, in yet another example of the kindness that Ohshiro was to encounter and to cherish over his life.

Through the Old Teacher's Eyes

I decided to make a special trip to Okinawa from Los Angeles. Once there, I found myself looking out over Naha city through the window of the lobby of a hilltop hotel. It was clear that another typhoon, so common in Okinawa, was approaching. The wind was strong and light rain had been falling since the previous day. But it was a welcome rain, for it took the edge off the muggy summer heat.

At the allotted time, Hirayama, Ohshiro's old teacher, arrived with his wife. In fact he taught me too and I also owe him a debt of gratitude. Unlike Ohshiro, however, I was a poor student, so I did feel a twinge of embarrassment at seeing him again. Hirayama was now 80 years old and a respected scholar of Okinawan classical literature. He was lecturing part-time at a university, and also taught ryuka, Okinawan folk poetry, at a few classes in Naha city. Ryuka is a compilation of Okinawan classical poetry, comparable to the Manyoshu collection of eighth century waka poetry from mainland Japan. Hirayama also held many more positions, could boast of many more achievements. He was a slim man, an expert in traditional martial arts, still practicing in fact. He was the very picture of health.

I decided to get straight to the point. "What was

Ohshiro like as a student?"

"Well," said Hirayama, closing his eyes and choosing each word carefully. "It will take time to talk about Hironari. There's a lot to say. He often visited me at home, and he lodged with my aunt for a long time". He then listed a number of students with whom Hironari had been close. "We were more like friends", he said. "Hironari always tried his very best, he had a good heart". His eyes shone as he spoke; as if he had shared something of Oshiro's compassionate nature, or perhaps of his struggle, and was pleased to see how the boy had turned out.

A person's expression can say much more than their words. It was clear that Hirayama's eyes were seeing far beyond the present, back half a century to the young boy he had taken under his wing. A boy who had done so well to leave his humble village and get to a school in the capital. A boy with whom he had shared meals and lodgings, a boy he had nurtured and inspired. To see how far he has come! Over the figure of Ohshiro, the successful businessman of today, Hirayama was layering his memories of Ohshiro, the boy of yesterday, with whom he had been so close. His eyes told me that he was still offering Ohshiro his support and still celebrating his student's success.

We finished lunch and wound up the interview, then got ready to leave. As we were about to part,

Hirayama wrapped up the mochi rice cakes, an Okinawan specialty, left uneaten on the table. "Take these with you", he said. I had been so busy listening to him reminisce that I had forgotten all about the mochi—normally my favorite. I was struck by his kindness. The same kindness with which he had nurtured the young Ohshiro.

We said goodbye in the hotel lobby, but walked together to the exit. I reluctantly climbed into my taxi. Hirayama and his wife waited in front the hotel, waving me off until the taxi was out of sight.

Despite his interest in continuing his education, the financial situation of Ohshiro's family meant that it was a dream never to be realized. He gave up on the idea of going to university and instead chose to set sail in the stormy waters of the business world.

In Naha, the light rain, signaling the typhoon, continued to fall, swirling and spiraling in the stormy winds.

Off to Tokyo through Mass Recruitment

It was 1960 when Ohshiro graduated from high school. A happy occasion, to be sure, but one which marked the beginning of a new set of challenges. It was Ohshiro's dream to go to the mainland, the capital, Tokyo City. At the time, there was one way of doing it that was much easier than any other. Mass recruitment. This was when groups of junior high school or high school graduates from Okinawa would be recruited, en masse, by a single company located on the mainland.

Back then, there was still a considerable gap in the standard of living between Okinawa and mainland Japan; a distance symbolized by the ocean between them. Most Okinawans simply did not have the financial resources to just up sticks and head for Tokyo. Ohshiro had been determined to go to Tokyo, but his group of graduates was recruited by a company in Nagoya, on the west coast of Japan, around 220 miles from Tokyo. So he began to plot a way to get from Nagoya to Tokyo. At Naha port, clutching his suitcase, Ohshiro boarded a ship bound for Kagoshima, then disappeared below deck.

Once he arrived in Nagoya, Ohshiro would start work at a company selling alcoholic drinks. It would be his first time on the mainland. When he arrived, he was confused and caught short by the many lifestyle and cultural differences. Work was tough; he was expected to solicit orders from his appointed sales area, but with cars still a relative novelty, he was forced to pedal his bicycle from house to house to make his sales calls. Once an order was placed, he then had to make the delivery. He made himself a trailer to attach to the back of his bicycle, which he would load up with heavy bottles of sake and soy sauce then set off to cover the dozens of miles on his delivery route. It was hard work but it paid enough for him to get some savings together. And it was here, in Nagoya, that Ohshiro got his first experience of making individual sales calls. Such sales calls are the fundamental principle of any network business. You can never tell where success will come in life.

Armed with his scant savings, Ohshiro moved from Nagoya to Tokyo. But he was not to be there for long.

Ohshiro got word that his father was in critical condition and immediately headed back to Nago. Once home, he started to work in the village office while taking care of his father. He worked in the tax collection department for seven years. How times have changed; he is the tax payer now, not the collector. Ohshiro found work in the village tedious. But he continued to dream, and eventually his desire for challenge would see him leave the village, once again, this time for good.

But life is not always all bad. His return from Tokyo to the village meant that he could reconnect with his childhood friend, Yaeko. She soon became his wife. And now, this loving couple has reached the heights of their success.

Chapter One:

Quenching the Thirst for Global Success,
From a Tiny Island to the World

Yes, I've done it, so you can too!

The island of Okinawa is beautiful to behold; brilliant white sands, seas sparkling with coral. It is a peaceful island, its western shores lapped by the waters of the Sea of China, its eastern coast caressed by Pacific Ocean waves. Seen on a globe it is no more than a pencil-dot in size, so small as to be almost unnoticeable. Fly over it and the islands will disappear from view in just a few short minutes. But the blue of the sky and the beauty of the sea will linger long in the memory. It takes more than five hours to fly from the west to the east coast of the United States. Okinawa is laughably small when compared to the great North American continent.

But spin that same globe around and you will see that, depending on how you look at it, any country can become the center of that globe. Every country is the center of the world to the people who live there. Spin the globe once more. An insignificant blob of land is now at the center of the world, while more impressive landmasses are cast to the far corners. How you see yourself as a part of the world as a whole will impact whether you win attention and affection or whether you are ostracized. How you choose to position yourself will determine the path you make through life.

Hironari Ohshiro, the man this book is about, always saw Okinawa as the center of the world, no matter how many times he spun the globe, no matter wherever else he went. He quenched his thirst for global success right from this tiny island.

In 2002, Ohshiro saw his dream take off to Tokyo. The next year, in 2003, he set up a small office in Los Angeles. Twelve years later, his business is active in the States, Canada, Mexico and a number of EU member countries, as well as in new markets in Asia and South America. He has now introduced Kangen

Water® to more than twenty national markets around the world.

1. Dreams, DREAMS, dreams

Dreams aren't for dreaming

"Dreams aren't for dreaming, they're for making come true". It's something Ohshiro often says. We cannot aim for success without having dreams in the first place. But many people see their dreams collapse and die. How big you dream is a reflection of how big you are. You cannot fit something large into something small. Everyone knows this to be the truth, and yet still, so often, this fundamental truth turns hollow when action is required. Having goals and working towards them is what enables us to gradually turn our small receptacle into something wider and deeper and large enough for our dreams.

Akio Morita and the men with whom he co-founded Sony had big dreams: to rebuild Japan and enrich its culture. Their endless energy meant that, after not too long, everyone in Japan—and, thanks to globalization, the world—had heard of their Sony. Steve Jobs, before his untimely death, had a dream: to make "a dent in the universe". A space-sized dream. He wanted his identity to leave a small yet palpable mark—a dent—in the universe. But has Jobs' stellar record of innovation and discovery really only left a dent, a fingertip-sized dimple, in our universe? He passed away while still young but the legacy of his boundless dream will surely never be forgotten.

It's been said that more than 90% of successful people have dreams and set goals. These aren't the sort of dreams that pop into your head by coincidence, unexpected ideas as random as the lottery. Deep down, everyone already knows this. We should have goals in life. We should be working toward those goals. Ohshiro did, and while there was much to overcome and many dues to pay, today he presides over a global company. It doesn't matter if you're from the tiniest island; you can still trade with the entire world. Your dreams are the propellers on which you can soar to success.

Tokyo-bound, once again

Ohshiro once again moved to the mainland, this time to take up an accountancy position in Tokyo. He was planning to become a certified public accountant but the flames that fired his entrepreneurial spirit still burned brightly. The young couple had quietly started to dream big for the future. These dreams prompted them first to make the move from Okinawa to Tokyo, then onwards to America. First the west coast, then the east. Then further still to Europe and beyond to Asia.

Even sharks can have amusing habits. Apparently sharks raised in aquariums never grow very large. But wild sharks, the sharks which swim freely in the open seas, can grow very large indeed. If Ohshiro had stayed in Okinawa, his growth might have been as stunted as a kept shark. Would he ever have managed to mature into a king of the international oceans? Think about the work of a gardener. To grow a big tree, first you must nurture the seeds in a small planting pot. Once the roots have extended far enough, the fledgling tree is transferred into a medium-sized pot, and then a larger pot, and so on. At last, the tree is given a new home in the ground where it can stretch out its branches as far as it might please. So even if you start off with something small, you should still be striving to make the receptacle holding that small and precious item as big as you possibly can.

So it was that Ohshiro and Yaeko made their way to the unknowns of the big city and all it had to offer.

Cramped city life

The Ohshiros firmly believed that success was to be found in Tokyo. They were ready to endure whatever hardships and difficulties live in the big city might involve and made their way back to its bright lights. Ohshiro was used to living in poverty. He was used to the struggle. The couple rented a small room in a little corner of Tokyo, with just enough space for the two of them to eat and sleep. Neither of them knew what life in Tokyo might hold. They had been prepared to put up with an extreme way of life when they decided to settle in Tokyo. But for Ohshiro, having Yaeko with him this time around gave him more strength and motivation than he could have hoped for. Any sadness or struggle could be shared— and therefore halved. Happiness, on the other hand, would double.

Ohshiro managed to find himself a job, but before long he was transferred to Osaka. He had always thought that he needed to be in Tokyo to see his dream come true, so inside he felt destroyed. But he could not turn his back on company orders, so off they went to Osaka. Not long after, however, the business employing him folded. Ohshiro felt an overwhelming sense of frustration, as everything he had been secretly agonizing about came rushing to the

surface. Why had he had ever had to leave Tokyo if the business was just going to fail? But he was not a man who was liked to show weakness.

"I am prepared to go anywhere, provided it be forward". These words were spoken by Dr. David Livingstone, a Scot who spent much of his life working as a missionary in Africa. His strength inspired him to say these words, while these words have inspired many others since.

2. Warm Spring Sunlight

A transformational encounter

Sometimes, in life, good can come out for misfortune. And for Ohshiro, his unlucky turn was to bring him together with someone very special indeed. One problem had been dealt with and waiting for him in Osaka was a man he did not yet know: Mr. Gushiken, President of the Sony sales branch in Osaka. Ohshiro's contact with President Gushiken was transformational: it would bring enough good fortune to drown out all of the difficulties he had suffered thus far. Life is all about who you meet. Ohshiro's life certainly changed direction with this particular meeting.

The warm spring sunlight is a gift from nature, a reward for enduring the long winter months. The energy from the sunlight stirs awake the living creatures which have spent the winter burrowed deep in the earth. I have seen the snows of Alaska; the year-long drifts, the midsummer snowfall. But the snow piles are melted by the summer sun and the flowers begin to push their buds up from the ground. The darkness of a tunnel is not everlasting. Drive on and soon you will see the light at its end.

Now, Ohshiro was enjoying the warmth of the spring sunlight. We should be grateful for the people we meet in life, for those encounters are not simply coincidence. My life here, now, too is a perhaps best described as a collection of all the people I have encountered thus far.

Last year, in around December, one of my friends sent me this wonderful poem, the author of which is unknown. It describes a journey on a train:

At birth, we boarded the train of life and met our parents, and we believed that they would always travel by our side. However, at some station, our parents would step down from the train, leaving us on life's journey alone.

As time goes by, some significant people will board the train: siblings, other children, friends, and even the love of our life.

Many will step down and leave a permanent

vacuum. Others will go so unnoticed that we won't realize that they vacated their seats! This train ride has been a mixture of joy, sorrow, fantasy, expectations, hellos, goodbyes, and farewells.

A successful journey consists of having a good relationship with all passengers, requiring that we give the best of ourselves. The mystery that prevails is that we do not know at which station we ourselves will step down. Thus, we must try to travel along the track of life in the best possible way — loving, forgiving, giving, and sharing.

When the time comes for us to step down and leave our seat empty — we should leave behind beautiful memories for those who continue to travel on the train of life.

Let's remember to thank our Creator for giving us life to participate in this journey.

I close by thanking you for being one of the passengers on my train!

1974: the birth of Sigmac Japan

The beam of light now illuminating Ohshiro—unemployed, unsure of what to do—was coming direct from President Gushiken. He was a veteran businessman, highly experienced in sales. Perhaps his interest in Ohshiro stemmed from their shared roots in Okinawa, but he gave the young Ohshiro some advice: go back to Okinawa and open a Sony sales branch there. Ohshiro had a feeling that the return of Okinawa to the control of mainland Japan, in 1972, would give a real boost to the islands' economy. From around two years before the handover, significant and historical changes had started to happen in Okinawa, in terms of the islands' relationship with the mainland, the economy, politics and even culture. Spurred on by President Gushiken's timely advice, Ohshiro began to dream a new dream: one in which the economic success of Okinawa brought economic success to him, too. So he established Sigmac Japan. Forty years have passed since then.

Sigmac Japan became an affiliated Sony sales retail store and sold a variety of products: Sony home electronics and home entertainment products, even Sony brand cosmetics. Sales were positive as the economy grew. The company quickly expanded, with sales channels spilling out over the ocean all the way to Kyushu, the southernmost main island of mainland Japan.

The business was built around making door-to-door sales calls. Ohshiro's first job had been when he was recruited as a door-to-door salesman by a brewery in Nagoya. Now, he was running a business based on the same sales model, only this time he was under the umbrella of business giant Sony. An irony of fate, perhaps. This period of his life also became the foundational stone upon which Ohshiro built his later success. In life, sometimes the ingredients for success can come tumbling onto our path from the most unexpected places. We just don't always notice straight away. But some of us are quick to realize that there are some diamonds among the stones which drop into our path.

At that time, Sony was a domestic brand and was a long way from achieving the sort of international recognition it has today. There was strong domestic demand and in any case Japan was enjoying an unprecedented economic expansion, the so-called Izanagi Boom. Hosting the summer Olympics in Tokyo in 1964 had only served to boost the economy further, and the boom was powered by what people called the 3Cs: cars, coolers, and color TVs. The whole country was racing furiously to try and catch up with the economy of its big brother, the US.

Losing the video tape wars

In 1970s, rapid innovation in the technology used to make home electronics created a brand new and ever expanding market. Corporate giants like Sony,

Matsushita, Toshiba and Hitachi went head-to-head in a battle to capture markets in Japan and overseas.

Ohshiro could already boast the top sales results of all Sony affiliated sales businesses in the Kyushu block, with annual revenue of 50 billion yen and 300 employees. Sigmac Japan was number one in the Kyushu block and Ohshiro was rewarded with an invitation to go to the US on a tour of inspection— meaning visiting Sony affiliates and some sightseeing, too. He still speaks with great emotion at the old America, the America he first saw on that trip, 35 years ago. They travelled across the States, visiting Nashville in Tennessee, San Diego in California, then Los Angeles. So it seemed certain that he had at last achieved success as a sales representative for Sony.

But fate was to be cruel once more and Ohshiro would soon be back to the struggle. His downfall was at the hands of the video tape wars: Betamax versus VHS. Sony refused to heed the call of the home electronics industry to work together to standardize video players, instead choosing to embark on an independent sales strategy. They took the opposite stance to Matsushita, Hitachi and all other companies manufacturing the VHS format. In the end, as we already know, Sony suffered a crushing defeat. The VHS format became the industry standard and Sony was left for dead in a booming market. Perhaps it had been arrogant of Sony. But the people who really suffered were the sales businesses located throughout Japan. Including, of course, Ohshiro and Sigmac Japan.

Sony introduced the Betamax videocassette magnetic tape recording format to the consumer market in 1975, while Matsushita launched the VHS format at around the same time. The Betamax format piggybacked on the strong reputation of Sony by promising high-quality imaging, to which Matsushita responded with the more reasonably priced VHS format. The market chose to go with the cheaper option, meaning that Sony lost out. The impact of the loss was felt throughout the whole of Sony, not just its video deck business. For Ohshiro, previously so successful that he had been invited on a business trip to America, the shock was so great that he was forced to close down his entire company. It was a hard lesson to learn for the young entrepreneur.

The aftershocks of the defeat took a long time to die down. Debts had to be repaid. But no matter how hard he worked or how much money he made, the debts just kept on piling up. Every repayment was nothing more than a drop in the ocean of debt that now surrounded him. Stories of Ohshiro's struggles began to spread round his home town.

Koichiro Higa, a man who has shared the last 40 years of struggle and success with Ohshiro and remains a key Enagic Group executive today, describes the mindset of his friend at the time as follows: "He was in big trouble. He had been backed into corner with no way to move forward and no way out. He was staring down into a tunnel of blackness, with no light to be seen at the end of it. He was in the depths of despair, unable to comprehend what had happened to his dreams. He was forced to close down his company, he had no other options. Closing the company meant making staff redundant, which in turn meant a heavy impact on their families, too. But Ohshiro could do nothing other than shut it down and start out on the search for something new. He had never before experienced such psychological pain. In the end, he tried to escape from it by flying back to Tokyo".

Today, many years later, Ohshiro often refers to his success and then failure with Sony when lecturing on entrepreneurship. After all, he is still putting the business methods he learned back then into use today within Enagic. Enagic is the new name for his old company, Sigmac Japan, and the fundamental principle for this new company remains network sales. Customers are called "distributors", even individual customers. Enagic adopts an approach similar to that taken by Sony in the early days, and Ohshiro's background with the company is the reason why.

A cold and wintry Tokyo greeted Ohshiro on his

return. It was much bleaker than the Okinawan winter cold. Yaeko, his wife, worked in a cafe, sometimes long into the night, to try and repay some of their debts. Ohshiro, too, threw himself into work, refusing to feel defeated. There was nothing to stop him building himself back up to the heights he had once reached. He just had to work hard. Neither of them could have imagined just how important these dark Tokyo days would be in generating the seeds for the success that was to come.

Near fatal shame

Ohshiro compares the failure and closure of his Sony sales business as comparable to his bout of malaria as a boy and the near-fatal injuries he suffered when hit by a military truck back in Nago. It was his third near-death experience. Closing the company, making his employees redundant, dealing with debt, having his assets seized. All this while his children were still so young. He felt himself lost in an angry sea, being driven to thoughts of suicide. It is a time he would rather not remember.

The closure of his company meant the destruction, from the roots up, of everything that he had worked so hard to build. The sort of solid foundation that could not be rebuilt in a day. His company had gone up in smoke and part of him wanted to disappear with it. Ohshiro describes the failure of his company as the "greatest shame a man could suffer". Japanese society is often said to be a culture of shame. Bankruptcy was the equivalent of a social burial. He could not face his fellow villagers. He could not face society. No bank would lend him a penny.

Ohshiro realized just how great a challenge he faced in setting up anew. The more he thought about what lay ahead, the more he began to think that his life was at an end. Nothing could comfort him, not even the thought that he had done nothing to warrant the failure—the fault lay with Sony's decision to market Betamax. His sense of crushing defeat, of humiliating failure, pushed him to ever more frequent thoughts of death.

But from within the depths of this despair, Ohshiro decided not to ignore his spirit of endurance, not to relinquish his dreams. Indeed, every time he was plunged into a cavern of desolation, the act of crawling out taught him how to live with strength and with fortitude. How to always fight on. How to always move forward. The fact that the business techniques he learnt at Sony are still used at Enagic, as it rapidly globalizes, surely says a lot about how he has learned from his past.

Some paths through life are fraught with struggle,

others with good fortune. Ohshiro had to use three of his lives before he finally struck lucky. He was soon to feel the warm spring sunlight again.

Destiny is a Kangen Water® seminar

Once year after closing the doors to Sigmac Japan, Ohshiro returned to Tokyo. But he wasn't simply running away from failure. He was once again feeling driven by his desire, unchanged from before, to realize his dream of success in the big city. Dreams aren't for dreaming; they are for making come true. That was Ohshiro's philosophy, and nothing could shake it from him. So however hard he might be knocked down, however long he might be knocked out for, he never had to struggle back up barehanded. He would find something to grasp onto, something that would lead him on the path to achieving his dreams. He was equipped with a natural instinct for survival.

In 1988, a seminar on Kangen Water® and its health benefits was held in Tokyo by a medical professor. An acquaintance recommended that they go along and listen, so Ohshiro agreed, reluctantly, to accompany him. At first, Ohshiro was skeptical—whatever this "Kangen Water®" that the professor was talking about, surely water was just water, you drank as much as you needed, and that was it. As the seminar progressed, however, Ohshiro began to realize that Kangen Water® was more than just the "ordinary" water that the Ministry of Health and Welfare told the people of Japan to drink. There were real benefits to the professor's water. And if a medical professor says it's true, how could it not be? The more he heard about the benefits of Kangen Water®, the more his interest grew. Later he would discover that Kangen Water® had already been recognized by the Ministry of Health and Welfare as having medicinal benefits. Ohshiro immediately set about learning more about Kangen Water®.

Ohshiro's success today is a direct result of his fateful decision to attend that seminar. Because that was when he first discovered the extent of the impact that Kangen Water® could have on the human body. It was the first time he heard that Kangen Water® was able to counteract the acidification of the human body caused by anti-oxidization. This was all new to him—but he understood it was important, too, so he took it all in, filed it all, and began to think about how he could turn it into a business. Ohshiro's animal-like instinct for sniffing out opportunities led him straight to his conclusion: this Kangen Water® could sell.

The seminar became the foundation stone upon which he was to build his dream for the future. It was the opportunity he could hardly have dreamed of. People say that life is about who you meet. In Ohshiro's case, his whole direction in life was turned upside down and about face by a seminar that he hadn't even wanted to go to. It was the opportunity that would make his dream of success in Tokyo come true. When you look at the process behind his success, it becomes harder to dismiss that success as the "magic of dreams", or "destiny" or even "mere coincidence".

It was Ohshiro's same animal-like instincts that allowed him to visualize how Kangen Water®, something he encountered for the very first time at that same seminar, could be turned into a business. As he listened to the professor talk, he started to calculate in his head. Who could supply the machinery, what was the market scope, who would be the target customers. Here was the moment of Enagic's birth, in the incubator of Ohshiro's mind. Business is all about stimuli: what you hear, see, say. Those stimuli must be turned into ideas, and then the ideas turned into cold, hard reality.

If we position it as the starting point for today's global Enagic business, it's hard to overstate the significance of this seminar. It's also perhaps why Enagic and its distributors hold seminars today; after all, the very top distributor learnt for himself just how transformational they can be.

The encounters we have in life can set us on

trajectories that we could never have imagined. Sometimes they take us down the wrong path, to unhappiness and bad fortune. Other times, they lead us to roads paved with riches. When Kazuo Inamori first set up Kyocera Corporation, in the 1960s, he attended a lecture, held in Kyoto, by Konosuke Matsushita, the founder of Panasonic. The theme of the lecture was "dam management". This was an approach to management that advocated maintaining a buffer, in other words, holding back (in a "dam") additional human resources, capital, and resources as insurance against change. Many of the attendees felt that, as a lecture from someone considered a giant of management, it had fallen somewhat flat. But Inamori was inspired: everything has to start from an idea, he thought. President Matsushita's "dam management" approach was to go on to have a significant impact on the management principles adopted at Kyocera Corporation.

Many other people would have been there too, at the lecture heard by Inamori and the seminar attended by Ohshiro. But how many of them managed to take what they had learned and use it to achieve business success? Even when it comes to knowledge that you hear from others, leaning with your ears, in other words, how you use that knowledge will depend on how you choose to listen and how you chose to learn from it.

Even if you're there in body, if you're not there in spirit then there is a risk that you will miss hearing about the really important things; they will go in one ear and straight out of the other.

3. The Dawn of Global Growth: 2003

The birth of Japan Enagic

Ohshiro had been given some very important insight at the seminar on Kangen Water® and health—and this insight didn't just apply to Japan. These issues with water and water quality applied to the entire world. Water is the foundation of health and if the water we take into our bodies is tainted then it's only natural that there are negative effects on our bodies. If we eat something bad, we get sick. Our health is dependent on what we consume. "I am what I eat". It's nothing more than common sense.

But the seminar didn't just talk about water quality. It also taught Ohshiro about the different types of water. Of course, Ohshiro had never heard that were or even considered that there might be different types of water. It was a revelation. He learned that the type of water we ingest can have just as much impact on our bodies as the quality of our water. Acidic water, kangen (alkaline) water, clean water. Each type has a different pH, each has a different purpose.

Ohshiro was almost sick of hearing how the health industry was going to be the big thing for the twenty first century. It was during the time when "wellness" was becoming a buzzword among executives of many companies in the USA. Once a society has become wealthy, people begin to spend increasing amounts of money on themselves: their face, their hair, right down to the toes on their feet. Ohshiro realized that Kangen Water® offered a chance for people to keep their health in balance. His business plan was starting to take shape.

First, Ohshiro began by selling the equipment needed—an electrolysis machine—to make Kangen Water® back home in Okinawa. His business strategy was once again based on the door-to-door sales techniques he had learnt over the course of his career. He ran the business this way for 5 or 6 years. The response was lukewarm; certainly not enough to satisfy Ohshiro. He decided, on instinct, that the business was better suited to an urban market and started, once again, to plan for a return to Tokyo. His dreams were still in Tokyo, he could not shake that conviction. So, once more, he left the island for the mainland.

Ohshiro and Yaeko set up a small office in Shinagawa. This was their first step along the path to the dream of Tokyo success. They say that even a journey of a thousand miles must begin with a single step. But they certainly had a long way ahead of them, not least the question of how to tackle a market of more than thirteen million people. Opening a retail store would require a significant capital investment: deposits for rent, building up stock, and plenty of other costs besides. But Ohshiro had returned to Tokyo still saddled with the after-effects of winding up his Sony business. Even so, he felt that Tokyo was his opportunity to break into a massive market. And you don't always need money to make the most of opportunity.

After mulling over his options, Ohshiro decided to once again adopt a door-to-door sales approach; it was an approach he knew well, after all. This method meant that products were sold direct from the manufacturer to the consumer, allowing him to frogleap over the margins taken by middle men and the complicated two-fold, three-fold distribution infrastructure that had taken hold of most industries in Japan. It also meant that the inevitable fixed cost of staff could be kept to a minimum too. This means big cost savings. All he had to do was add his margin to the profit taken by the sales agent and he would have an exciting product with a decent margin. This firm belief was the fuel he needed to push forward with his sales. It was also to become the foundation of his "eight point system", which will be introduced later.

So, in 1997, Sigmac Japan transformed into Enagic Co., Ltd., and Ohshiro set about gaining himself a foothold in the wellbeing market using his new sales approach.

Japan Enagic's rapid rise

Ohshiro's conviction, and the way he set about making it happen, both proved spot-on. Month on month, sales of Kangen Water® machines were rising. Sales were better than even Ohshiro expected; he was, at last, inching towards realizing his Tokyo dream. His margin was reasonable, his profit beginning to emerge. He moved his office to a more central location, by Tokyo Station, and opened branches from Sapporo in the north of Japan to Naha back home in Okinawa. Those around him look back at that time and describe the momentum of business growth as being as fast as the bullet that shoots a bird from the sky. The Enagic kangen machine, conceived on a tiny island, was now making itself known around the whole of Japan.

A few years later, while sales of kangen machines were still growing, Ohshiro decided that he needed to immediately secure a manufacturing facility to produce these machines. If he was going to take the business overseas, he would need to be able to guarantee production and make his supply stable. So he set out to buy one of the plants where the machines were being produced from his supplier. He succeeded in acquiring a plant in Osaka and promptly renamed it Toyo Aitex. This was the predecessor of the current Enagic plant.

The decision to buy a production plant had a significant transformational impact on the sales system within Enagic. First, demand and supply needed to be stabilized. Quality assurance, private branding, and corporate reputation management all needed to be secured, too. Bringing production in-house generates a number of synergistic effects: some visible, some invisible. Sales continued to be healthy after the purchase of the plant, enough to support growing demand, manufacturing at full blast. At the same time, the company began to reach beyond Japan and expand into export markets.

Brushing off executive resistance

With his domestic sales framework now firmly in place and production brought in-house, Ohshiro, spurred on by his dream of success in Tokyo, began to look at international markets. He had already expanded his market base from Okinawa to Tokyo;

now it was time to stretch it from Tokyo all the way to Los Angeles.

Los Angeles is a leading city on the west coast of the United States, and if Ohshiro could get a footing in LA, from there he could set his sights on the east coast, too. And once he was set up on the east coast, beyond the Atlantic lay another huge opportunity: the EU. Ohshiro's dream of making a success of things in Tokyo was gradually beginning to take wing and soar across the seas.

Initially, some of the executives opposed Ohshiro's plan to launch into the US market. At the Tokyo headquarters, plans were put in place to expand into the LA market. First, he appointed a manager with the necessary English skills and named him branch manager. He asked an acquaintance who was a lawyer to accompany him to LA, where they would start making contacts with a view to scoping out the local market. He was researching the market and making preparations to launch in LA.

However, Ohshiro heard a rumor that one of his old classmates from Naha Commercial High School was living in the city and had been serving as a pastor and management consultant for many years. It was just the connection he needed, so Ohshiro determined to check out this classmate. So he visited one of his old high school teachers, who had also taught the classmate. This is how I came to be involved in the dawn of Enagic's global expansion, how I came to be a liaison for Ohshiro's ventures in the States. It was thirteen years ago.

An old teacher's hunch

Here I would like to introduce another of our old teachers, Reverend Yasumasa Unten. Forty years passed before that fateful reunion with Ohshiro. Rev. Unten was another teacher who had left a strong impression on the young Ohshiro. He has been serving as a pastor for over 50 years, but in his twenties he was a high school teacher, after which he became an instructor at the University of the Ryukyus. It was this connection with Rev. Unten that led to Ohshiro and I working together in Los Angeles. Without this connection, perhaps we would both have walked two different paths, without ever crossing.

In the course of writing this book, I flew to Okinawa to speak with Rev. Unten. I still think of him as my teacher, but I also take pride in the fact that I am one of the people who can tell what he is really thinking. Without any prelude, I got stuck straight into the interview: "What kind of schoolboy was Ohshiro?"

"Quite a few boys studied with me in preparation

to go to university. But Ohshiro was different from all of them". That was the first thing to come from Rev. Unten's lips.

"Different how?" I asked.

"He was polite and a very good student", he said, gradually getting into the topic. "He was a good communicator. I felt that he had something of a grand scale about him". Suddenly, he looked resolute. "He was definitely cut out to be a businessman".

I had the comment I had been looking for. We both shared our happiness at Ohshiro's success. At that moment, Unten's wife interrupted with some words from the Book of Job in the Old Testament:

Though thy beginning was small,
yet thy latter end should greatly increase.

"Tiny streams merge into great rivers", she concluded. We set off together for dinner, arranged by their first son Hiroki, and there I said a toast, to the health of my old teacher and his wife, and to the success of my old school friend.

The 43 year reunion

One day in January 2003, I headed to Los Angeles International Airport and waited in the arrivals lobby. They quickly appeared: Ohshiro and his wife Yaeko.

They had passed through immigration and came out beaming. At first I wondered if I was greeting the wrong person. Ohshiro had a full, thick head of dark hair, and his face was smooth; he looked like a man still in his forties. Perhaps it was the gap of forty-odd years between our last meeting and this moment that made me so conscious of his appearance. So whether it was because I was so struck by his youthful looks, I didn't find out about his considerable success until much later.

It had been 43 years since we both graduated from high school in 1960. In school, our interests had been different and we hadn't really spoken. Still, I had remembered him as a committed student. He always had his school books in his hands; he was always studying after school. I could only feel that meeting him again like this was the result of God's divine guidance.

Ohshiro was quick to get down to work. Once settled in his hotel in Beverly Hills, his first trip was to my house, to set up a Kangen Water® system and test it out. He was checking the quality of the water in Los Angeles, how the taps and the kitchen counters were fitted. Ever since that day, I have been drinking Kangen Water® and I continue to be amazed by its effects.

A speedy local start

"Do it fast, even if it may be a mistake." It might sound a little strange, but it is a core principle for Ohshiro. If it's a mistake, you can fix it later. Whether it's also because he is impatient, the fact is that he doesn't want to see any opportunities lost. You need to make a pre-emptive strike before anyone else has a chance to grab onto the opportunity you have discovered.

For Ohshiro, that meant heading straight to my office from the airport and immediately setting up a local corporation under Californian state law. The next day, the three of us headed to downtown LA to register the new company. Next we set up an interim office, hired a member of staff, and that was enough to get Enagic USA, Inc. going officially.

At the end of June in that same year, Ohshiro gave his first seminar as President of Enagic USA, in the Torrance Holiday Inn. Around eighty people attended. Among them were some of the top distributors of Enagic products in Japan.

A few weeks later, I was woken by the phone ringing at one in the morning. The ring sounded so much louder in the nighttime quiet. I picked it up.

"We need to set up an office and get it up and running in Hawaii within the next three weeks". It was a call from a manager in charge of the US. This was going to be tight. I flew to Hawaii immediately. I had lived on the island for three and a half years, so I had plenty of friends and acquaintances. I started to get back in touch with my Hawaiian network, and within two or three days had registered a branch, leased an office, got in touch with accountants and lawyers. The Hawaiian office opened for business in September 2003.

"Do it fast, even if it's a mistake." This same principle has been the driving force behind a flurry of expansion, the growth of a network of sales branches across the globe: Los Angeles, Hawaii, New York, Chicago, Vancouver, Mexico, Texas, Washington State, Florida. And in between, Hong Kong. Then the EU: Germany and France. Then back to Asia again. All in just twelve short years.

This is why it's fair to say that Enagic and its kangen machine have achieved globalization in a single stroke. I have been involved in setting up a great number of new companies, but never before or since have I seen such immediate and exponential growth. Ohshiro might have come from a tiny island, but he certainly managed to quench his thirst for global success.

Americans think of Los Angeles as a city that turns people from nobodies into somebodies. I've lived in LA for 43 years, so I can tell you that it's true. There's a saying I often hear and it goes like this:

> Go to LA if you want to be somebody
> Go to New York if you are somebody
> Go to Florida if you want to be someone else

Once again, it seems that Ohshiro's animal instincts brought him to just the right place.

4. Globalization: Quenching the Thirst for Global Success

This will never sell!

There's another story to tell about the setting up of the first international Enagic company in LA. Many of the top distributors in Japan sensed the opportunity that the west coast represented and asked the company to give them exclusive rights to sell Enagic products. LA is not unlike the other side of the river bank from Japan. Many Japanese people have an existing network here: family, relatives, friends, students, corporate connections. It's a city filled with dynamic small and medium-sized enterprises run by entrepreneurs of many different ethnicities. Ohshiro couldn't allow the huge potential of this market to be lost to someone else. So he opened Enagic USA with the backing of a wealth of ambitious, entrepreneurial distributors.

Ten years ago, most potential buyers thought that Enagic products were too expensive. The most popular product in Japan retailed for 360,000 yen. Ohshiro wanted to sell the same product for $3,600. There was disagreement and in the end the price was lowered to $2,900. Sales started to rise rapidly, month on month. Two years later, Ohshiro was able to sell the product at the price he had originally set.

Today, imitation and ostensibly similar products have become available. It's a clear sign that Enagic products remain head and shoulders above the rest.

Locking targets on Asia

Ohshiro was very aware that he was not on home territory and kept his sales strategy conservative. He couldn't afford to make a mess of his first overseas endeavor. In the first instance, since his company was Japanese, he chose Los Angeles, a city with a large Japanese population, and targeted Japanese ex-pats and second-generation Japanese as his core targets. Gradually, he expanded his targets to include Americans of Korean, Chinese, Filipino, and Mexican descent, before moving on to white and black Americans. He focused on Koreans and second-generation Koreans in particular, often using hotels in

Korean Town to hold seminars. Even with this Korean market there were cultural differences and business differences, which meant that the products were not always well received. Misunderstandings were had, mistakes were made. Still, he was able to establish a strong base within the local Korean market, which then allowed for expansion. In New York, he expanded his focus to include Christian groups and Central and Middle American ethnicities; these communities began to respond to our products without us targeting them specifically. It is not always easy to run a business in markets that are multi-ethnic, multi-lingual, multi-cultural. Some of the staff, unused to these cultural differences, were sent spinning. Differences in ethnicity were also reflected in product knowledge, credit-based sales, recalls, and service. Ohshiro would need to learn more about managing a business in a global city.

But while problems remained, they weren't enough to stop the company's steady growth.

Creating a global product

Kangen Water® machines are loved in the most unexpected of markets. Alaska, the northernmost state in America; Denmark, in northern Europe; Cape Town in South Africa. Enagic machines have even found their way to Mauritius, a tiny island next to Madagascar, which lies off the coast of East Africa. We had never even heard of the island until we came to have a connection with it through Kangen Water® machines. The brand is present on many other islands, too: in the Caribbean alone our machines are used in Puerto Rico, Jamaica, Trinidad and Tobago. In South America we have a sales branch in Brazil and our products have moved into the Argentine and Paraguay markets. It surely won't be long too until Enagic products make their way all the way to the south of Peru, down by the Antarctic.

So where does the appeal of Enagic products lie? There are great discrepancies between economic zones, great differences living environments. Yet the popularity of Enagic products—admittedly high in cost—remains reasonably high. It's said that the average income in Southeast Asia is just one seventh of average American income. And one US dollar is worth about 3.5 times a Malaysian Ringgit, for example. The exchange rate is not necessarily a reflection of the value of money, but even after factoring in aspects of living standards, the fact remains that a Kangen Water® ionizer is an expensive outlay. Yet in Southeast Asia, the products are picking up in popularity. That's because being expensive isn't enough to stop a product from selling. Achievements are still to be had in countries with weak economies: the way you structure and adapt your business will provide the foundation for success. Everyone needs a car; you can choose to pay $15,000 for a low-end model or $100,000 for a luxury ride. Enagic's pride in its products as the "luxury cars" of the wellbeing market is key to enhancing their marketability.

Hong Kong: the gateway to a giant market

It wouldn't be right to talk about the globalization of Enagic without mentioning Hong Kong. A city I long dreamed of visiting one day. At last, I was able to make the trip Hong Kong Airport, much bigger than I had expected, is a sight to behold. In September 2014, Hong Kong university students launched a movement to protest the proposed reforms to the system in place for electing the Chief Executive of Hong Kong in time for the 2017 election. I am deeply interested in the history of Hong Kong. My sense is that this student movement has taken China a step closer to democratization.

Hong Kong always makes me think back to a certain period in history; 1840, around the time of the Opium War between Great Britain and Qing China. In China, smoking opium had become common since long before the advent of the Qing dynasty; Britain started to smuggle opium into China from India, a British colony at the time. History tells us that the smuggling was in order to force a trade imbalance with Qing China, to accumulate capital through industrial revolution, and to raise funds for the War of Independence in the States. The end result of the war was that Hong Kong became a British crown colony.

Hong Kong was under British control for 99 years; in 1997, sovereignty was once again transferred to the People's Republic of China. Much of the global population—and of course of Hong Kong—was anxious about the direction the governance of HK might take; the handover prompted a significant number of Hong Kong residents to emigrate to Canada. But the Chinese politicians were wily; they introduced the "one country, two systems" principle. One head, controlling two bodies. China and Hong Kong, one and the same country. But one with two political systems, with Hong Kong keeping its administration for the time being. It is commonly understood that the "one country, two systems" principle can remain untouched for 50 years after reunification. But there's no chance the Chinese government will just be sitting there, waiting, doing nothing, for that half century. The current Chinese administration will doubtless do anything and everything they can to gain the upper hand.

The rest of the world wants to see democracy take root in China. Nearly 20% of the world's entire population lives in China. It is an enormous market, so big you would have to group several other countries together to match it. While it has not sustained the stupendous growth earlier recorded, it is still increasing steadily, albeit at a slower pace. If the country becomes democratized, then we will doubtless see a loosening of certain policies, including business regulations. The networking business approach is new to China; this alone is enough for us to wish to democracy.

It's still not clear what impact these student demonstrations will have on the authoritarian political environment in China. What it sure is that the demonstrations captured the world's attention. Surely the calls for Chinese democratization and liberalization can only become ever greater, ever louder.

Enagic Hong Kong: getting our foot in the door of Asia

This was how I felt on the ride from Hong Kong International Airport to my hotel. From the window of my taxi, I gazed out at all the construction: the highways, the skyscrapers.

It felt like a vibrant hive of economic activity. At the hotel, I was met by an Enagic staff member, who talked me through the schedule for the day. We visited the office just after five. For around two hours, the Hong Kong sales branch manager and the Asia Regional Manager explained their operations to me. By the end of the meeting, we had managed to hash out an image of what we wanted for the first Hong Kong branch. I was pretty impressed with the way they had been conducting Enagic business here in Hong Kong.

Whenever Ohshiro comes to the States, he always speaks proudly of business in Hong Kong. How we should all look to Hong Kong as a model for the business. At his monthly meetings in the States, he emphasizes how attentive the Hong Kong staff are toward customers and how strong their business performance is. He tries to motivate the Enagic staff in Los Angeles, to have them feel a little jealousy and a renewed sense of "well, we'll show them". But would stirring up competition be of any use?

Perhaps it's the norm in Hong Kong, but the office will still be crammed with customers at seven in the evening. The staff are busy looking after the customers; no-one is tidying up or trying to get home, even if office hours are officially over. In the States, nobody is in the office outside of their allotted shifts. I can sense the same "vibe" that I felt on the way from the airport to the hotel in the Enagic office too. Hong Kong is still enjoying a period of economy growth, so I don't want to jump to conclusions about whether this is due to national characteristics or just the energy of this particular office. Of course, I realized why Ohshiro was so gushing about Hong Kong. I'd heard him say it in Los Angeles, but it was indeed true: once you've felt it and seen it, you know that the Hong Kong vibe is something special.

When I got back to my hotel room, there was a

water bag in the room, filled with Kangen Water®. When you're used to drinking Kangen Water®, it can be hard to access the water when travelling; you never know when you will be able to replenish your supply. My roommate and I were impressed with the attentiveness, the preparedness of the Hong Kong branch staff. I felt myself agreeing with Ohshiro: it's not surprising that sales are good if this is the way they interact with their customers.

It has been ten years since the Hong Kong branch was opened. Now, it will be the foot that holds open the door to the vast Asian market. Many Enagic branches have used and will continue to use Hong Kong as a gateway, from which to divide and multiply the number of distributors throughout Asia. Changed see above!!

But Ohshiro has confessed to me that, out of frustration at the branch's slow progress, "at one time, I thought about closing it". But now, the very branch which was under threat of closure has blossomed into a beautiful flower that is spreading its branches across Asia.

A millionaire rush

Apple Corporation, in Silicon Valley, is well known for being a company which has generated many millionaires through the opportunities it gives to employees via a profit sharing system. Enagic is not at a comparable scale, but thanks to its unique commission-based system, it has produced a few. One distributor, who used to work for a competitor but then started to work for Enagic, has spoken of how his earnings are incomparable to what they were before. Another distributor was unemployed and unable to meet his house and car repayments, until, clutching at straws, he started to work for Enagic; within six months he was earning handsome commissions. The commissions our distributors can earned have helped with crippling medical bills, or brought people back from the brink of financial ruins, or even helped to mend marriages. It has meant the realization of financial health, physical health, mental health. Of course, the same can perhaps be said for other companies. But Enagic is distinct: in its contribution, its speed, and its immediate effect. The capital required to get going is low, there's no need to maintain a large inventory, there's no sales targets to meet. There are definite merits here: our distributors manage themselves, aren't bound by top-down restrictions, and can expand their business freely.

One of our distributors, Eli Dafesh, describes his experiences with Enagic as follows:

I fear my words will not do this incredible man

the justice that he deserves and that no matter what I might say, it would fall short of truly explaining the honor and privilege it has been to know Mr. Ohshiro. But I was asked to make this contribution, so I will do my best. My first exposure to Enagic was in 2006, at an event on the Queen Mary in Long Beach, CA. Mr. Ohshiro was giving a presentation to a packed house, mainly of Japanese people. He gave his talk in Japanese, with an English interrupter doing his best to keep up with him. While I tried my best to listen to the English version of the information, I was captivated by the passion and conviction of the man speaking. Although I could not understand the language he was speaking, I understood every feeling he uttered. Any language barrier that may have existed at first crumbled and I quickly realized that this man, Hironari Ohshiro, and I were kindred spirits, men that shared a burning desire to succeed and to help others. I immediately knew I wanted to meet and work with this man.

When I first meet Mr. Ohshiro I had already been very successful in business. I had worked in the beauty salon industry for over 20 years and then had tried my hand in the network marketing / direct sales industry, where I became a one million dollar-plus annual earner and a trainer. My experience had taught me to recognize opportunity and potential, but perhaps even more importantly, it taught me to recognize leadership. This is one area that is often lacking in traditional Network Marketing businesses. Making a lot of money and driving expensive cars and wearing flashy clothes and jewelry are not the signs of leadership. Instead, true leadership is often soft spoken and subtle; it somehow finds its way through all the hype and the cheers. Mr. Ohshiro was the embodiment of leadership, which was one of the things that impressed me most about him. Once I got to know Mr. Ohshiro on a more personal level, he ended up being just as passionate, as driven, as committed as I had thought he was.

It is said that you can tell a lot about a man based on the way he treats his wife. If this is true, then Mr. Ohshiro would be a thoughtful, respectful, faithful and honorable man, which he is. They are an incredible couple, at each other's sides almost all of the time. It has been a pleasure to get to know both of them, and my wife, Jillina, and I consider Mr. & Mrs. Ohshiro as very dear friends.

My life, and the life of my family, has been impacted beyond words by working with Mr. Ohshiro. The incredible products and the unbelievable opportunity of Enagic have created a lifestyle that most cannot even comprehend. It has allowed us one of the most sought after assets available: freedom of time. Of course, we also enjoy a beautiful home and all the luxuries that come with financial success, but frankly, without freedom of time, everything else ends up being pretty insignificant. If you don't have time to enjoy the fruits of your labor with those you love, what is the point? This is a lesson that Mr. Ohshiro has embedded in my mind. Although he has made vast fortunes, he lives very simply and is always looking for ways that he can help others. He has set an incredible example, worthy of being followed by anyone.

Mr Ohshiro has honored me and my family with your compassion, your wisdom, your generosity, your spirit and your love. To show my appreciation I have done my best to be a good husband, a good father, a good distributor, and a good mentor. I humbly thank you for the incredible opportunity you have created for me and so many others and the amazing good fortune you have bestowed on my entire family. Words cannot express the depth of my heartfelt thanks, but I hope you know how much I appreciate all you have done for me and my family.

A million global distributors

Today, there are more than 650,000 Enagic distributors around in world. The "kangen water from Okinawa" that Ohshiro started with his wife, Yaeko, started selling by themselves has now traversed oceans, soared over mountains, crossed borders, and got over cultural and linguistic differences, to become a water that is drunk and loved by families all over the world. And its momentum continues to increase, month in, month out.

A look back at how the business has expanded globally and into new markets up until now suggests that within four or five years, Enagic will have one million distributors worldwide. Enagic has a very strong growth rate. It was only twelve years ago that the business moved into the US, and as of now Enagic already has 200,000 distributors. Sales in the EU market are growing steadily and performance in Asian countries is a sight to behold. Customs change with countries, and it's true that the way distributors are handled does differ according to their countries. It's certainly not easy managing so many distributors adequately. For example, Malaysia is a Muslim country, which means that lease agreements must be adjusted to allow distributors the space to conduct religious activities. Some countries have no notion of freedom of choice in religion. In Italy, for example, long lunch breaks, known as "riposo", of 3-4 hours are taken, but then work continues until late at night. The idea that wine can be cheaper than water is something which doesn't make intuitive sense to the Japanese.

It's easy to bundle everything together into the term "global business", but this must be backed by an exacting framework of management, administration, human resources management, and strategy.

Our 650,000 distributors comprise people of many different ethnicities: Asians, Caucasians, black people, Hispanics, Latin Americans, ethnic minorities. Even within the States, there can be cultural differences between white and black Americans. And there can be big differences between Americans of Japanese descent and native Japanese. Enagic is showing strong growth in the face of the world's dynamic population. Enagic continues to have an economic impact on individuals and bring about significant changes to their lifestyles. It will not be long before one million distributors are aboard the SS Enagic, as it sails across the ocean seas to further success.

Today, Enagic products are exported to more than 120 countries worldwide.

Okinawa Global Convention

In June 2013, Ohshiro was planning something extravagant. He would invite the world's top performing distributors to the village of his birth, Setake. But would anyone really come all the way to a tiny village in Okinawa? His closest staff were worried. From France, for example, a distributor would have to fly from Paris to Narita Airport in Tokyo, then onwards to Naha International Airport, then stay in a hotel in Naha or its surroundings, before getting on a bus for several hours to get to Setake. The logistics of travel alone would involve considerable time and distance. And money, of course. But Ohshiro was insistent.

June 2013. One hot summer day followed another in Okinawa. The summer heat of Okinawa is often described as being similar to having a steam bath. You have to have several handkerchiefs in your pocket if you want to get through the day. It's so hot that you can even break into a sweat just sitting down. The Global Convention was held in the old gym hall of the building that used to house Ohshiro's elementary school. The venue had no air conditioning, so a mobile air conditioning unit was temporarily installed. The gym hall was jam packed with 800 of the top distributors from Japan and the rest of the world and the air was filled with their energy—and their sweat.

One by one, in that hot, sweaty hall, the attendees introduced their own success stories: smiling, they talked about their first encounter with kangen water, how it had benefited their health and their personal finances, how it had brought them success. At the end of their speeches, Ohshiro gave a key note speech: "Have Goals". The convention was followed by a dinner, where the attendees enjoying delicious Okinawa food, all the while wiping the sweat from their brows. People from all over the world, enjoying Okinawan food in a sleepy village. Surely this was the very realization of Ohshiro's biggest dream.

From outside, the scene was striking: the bright colors of eighteen different national flags, flapping together in the evening wind. People from across the globe, all together now in this remote corner. People speaking English, French, Spanish, Chinese. It was a festival of international culture. What on earth had been the attraction? What sense of obligation had prompted all these people to spend such time and money getting to a place like this? It may well seem strange. But what did the residents of Ohshiro's old village see that night?

I was entranced by the sight of the villagers dancing Okinawan folk dance under the flags of the world and the voices of those Eisa dancers echoing across the night. I felt as if I were in a dream; surely this is what it means to quench the thirst for global success.

40th Anniversary Global Convention

Enagic, as the new incarnation of Sigmac Japan, was celebrating its fortieth year of business. Should the venue be in Tokyo or Los Angeles? The key to the decision was strategic thinking. Holding it in Tokyo would mean great transport links, but Los Angeles or Las Vegas would mean 4,000-5,000 distributors in immediate range. Choose the west coast, and plenty of distributors would likely come from Southeast Asia to mix business with the pleasure of tourism. But Ohshiro decided that the fortieth anniversary of Enagic should be held in a place that celebrated where the company originated.

Gradually, the top distributors from around the world began to arrive in Naha International Airport. Great Britain, France, Italy, the Middle East, Africa, Asia, the States, Canada, Mexico, South America; almost too many countries to count. Nearly a thousand distributors came, from the twenty countries where there are branches, from the 120 countries to which products are exported. The 40th Anniversary Global

Convention celebrated the Enagic's milestone with brilliance and bustle.

Many of the distributors took several flights to get to the convention. Peter Shaw, a distributor from the Netherlands, made his first trip to Okinawa. He is one of the many distributors who have been greatly inspired by his experiences. He had some words of congratulations, as follows:

It is always reassuring to have partners who are steady and reliable. I would like to offer my congratulations to Enagic and to President Ohshiro for the past forty years. Not many companies ever achieve such impressive results. For all of us, who have decided to build our careers in this industry, having such a steady and reliable partner is a great reassurance. I look forward to seeing this wonderful company change the lives of many millions more people, through its vision and its unending march forward.

(From the 40th Anniversary Global Convention program)

Words of congratulation poured in from distributors all over the world. How many other companies would be able to hold a global convention in Okinawa, of all places? I've never heard of such a thing, and I am from Okinawa myself. A man who has been so nearly broken by setback after setback cannot enjoy walking his glorious path without seeking to give hopes and dreams to others. Ohshiro walks along single path, but each distributor has the chance to carve out their own pathway to success.

Dreaming of the EU market

I have already introduced how Enagic made inroads into the US market, but the dream to launch onto the EU market broke free from its incubator during trips to New York and Washington DC, and began to toddle forward.

In 2004, we visited the New York branch to attend its opening seminar. We arrived at JFK International Airport then headed to the office in central Manhattan. The island, seen from the window of my taxi, was buried in under a mountain of white snow. It reminded me of the white sands of Okinawa. We had come so far; from a tiny island to this great city, New York, the beating heart of the world's economy.

The first seminar didn't attract many participants, perhaps because of the heavy snow. We finished the seminar and Ohshiro and the rest of his party immediately headed to LaGuardia airport to fly to Washington DC. He was used to travelling around the US, but it was to be his first time in Washington DC. And the next day, we would have the chance to catch a glimpse of the President of the United States, George

W. Bush. Ohshiro must have started to feel flustered. The man from the tiny island, standing in front of the White House. What dreams had he dreamt to bring him here?

We were staying at the historic Willard Intercontinental Hotel. The White House was just a stone's throw away. The hotel is renowned for having housed Abraham Lincoln in the weeks up to his inauguration. Today it is known as the "Residence of Presidents", the accommodation of choice for presidents and foreign dignitaries.

Around the time of the Meiji Restoration (1868), the government of Japan sent a group of civil servants on a diplomatic mission to various countries around the world. This Iwakura Mission visited Washington DC., and stayed in the Willard Intercontinental. The hotel still uses these historical guests as part of their PR. The Iwakura Mission was an ambassadorial mission, sent to visit American and various European countries. It comprised a number of prominent politicians and a group of students; the Willard Intercontinental welcomed them all. One of the stories from the mission goes like this:

The majority of the mission members wore Western clothes, but Tomomi Iwakura, the leader of the mission, continued to wear traditional Japanese clothes and style his hair in a traditional Japanese samurai style known as "mage". He was, however, given a talking to by his son, who had come on the mission with him, and he decided, in Chicago, to get a haircut and spent the rest of the mission in Western clothes.

The interpreter for the group had been a Japanese man named Joseph Hardy Neesima (his adopted Western name). On his return to Japan, he opened an English school, which was later to become the Christian university Doshisha University. Many of the men who were part of the Iwakura Mission are remembered today as prominent figures in the "civilization and enlightenment" period in Japan which followed the political change brought about by the Meiji Restoration. Men such as Hirobumi Ito, who would later become Prime Minister, and the politician and modernizer Toshimichi Okubo. The mission stayed in the States for eight months, then crossed the Atlantic to Europe.

The Willard Intercontinental, then, is an historic hotel, the temporary home of men who, dreaming of the Westernization of Japan, had come to visit so long ago. Of course, they would have stayed up all night talking, strategizing about the future of their country. For Ohshiro, too, his stay in this hotel proved fateful. For it was here he decided to broaden even further the scope of his dream to introduce kangen water to the

EU. Beyond the snow-covered White House lay the EU, and beyond that still, the Russian market.

Something came to him, from the snow-frosted White House and the chill of the thickly falling snow. Something that burned with a passion. And he was greatly looking forward to tomorrow's keynote speech from President George W. Bush.

Breakfast with Bush

The following day, an old friend, Takashi Uehara from school who was living in Washington DC came to meet Ohshiro. The friend had been an outstanding student at university; it had been hoped that he would stay on and teach there. But his dream for the future was to become a pastor, and he had dedicated himself to missionary work from a base in Washington DC. He guided us on our way from the hotel to the venue where we would be having breakfast with Bush.

The National Prayer Breakfast is an annual event, organized jointly by Christian members of both the Democratic and the Republican parties. It is a major international event in the Christian calendar, attended by leading figures from politics, finance, diplomacy, and the Christian faith. Around 2,250 guests from all over the world join together in a single venue. It is cramped, so monitors are set up in lobby and the hallways into which guests overflow. As special guests, we had a table reserved, and sat with political representatives from Texas and businessmen from Virginia; we enjoyed lively discussion about politics and business. Ohshiro held his own in the conversation, despite lacking confidence in his English. The conversation moved onto more personal topics. I asked my tablemates how old Ohshiro looked to them. "About 35, I suppose," said one young business woman at the table. I revealed his true age and the entire table was shocked; Ohshiro just smiled, gleefully. I've also heard that, very occasionally, at the end of distributor seminars when Ohshiro is leaving the venue, a distributor will tug at his hair from behind. Apparently they want to check whether he's actually wearing a wig.

The venue was truly international; we could hardly see a single Asian or Japanese person on any of the tables around us. We heard later that there had been eight guests from Japan in total.

As soon as President Bush appeared to give his keynote speech, a wave of excitement rushed through the venue; we greeted him with a standing ovation. A sign of respect from the whole country towards its President. The fact that leading figures from within and beyond the United States were welcoming this man with a standing ovation made it clear to me that I was witnessing, before my very own eyes, the power, the national might, of the States. The President was making this speech not long before the election that would determine whether he served a second term, but his message was politics-free. "Prayer makes us all equal before God". The President's words resonated deeply in my heart.

An international event that can invite the President of the United States as a guest serves to turn the attention of its guests to the States and to the world as well. For us, having come from a tiny island in the middle of the Pacific, it was a chance to witness the "global village" of the world. To see the world we had gazed out upon in Okinawa, this time from the States, from the leader of the world, allowed us to expand our perspective, to broaden it to new horizons.

To end this chapter, I would like to introduce Ohshiro's pride and joy: his private country golf course.

Building a golf course for his global distributors

Today, Enagic is active in 120 countries, through exports and sales of Enagic branded products. That total represents about 60% of the 193 countries which are members of the United Nations. From its origins in Okinawa, Enagic has become a global company both in name and in deed. While he was busy expanding his business around the world, Ohshiro also set his mind to building a golf course in the mountains near his hometown. It is a place of great scenic beauty, the Pacific Ocean stretching out to the east, lush green forests hugging the surrounding mountains. The course is extremely well-maintained, to the delight of its golfers, yet is also designed to be challenging. As those golfers who can't get good score on the books say jokingly, it's a reflection of Ohshiro's own personality.

The Enagic Golf Course was completed in June 2013, but the project took a great deal of time, energy and investment to get it up and running. It was built so that the distributors who come to visit Okinawa from all over the world would have somewhere to enjoy golf and to enjoy their vacation. Still, there's always plenty of time to talk business on the golf course. The course also helps to recharge the local economy, bringing prosperity to Ohshiro's home village.

At times, Ohshiro manages to pull quite unbelievable things off without breaking a sweat. The building and the operation of this golf course is one of those things. On the face of it, there is no clear connection between the kangen water business and running a golf course. So what's the point of the golf course? But Ohshiro sees things differently. A course where distributors from across the world can enjoy a game of golf at a bargain price. A private course, reserved for distributors only. An Enagic resort, where distributors can relax with their families, breath in the refreshing air of Okinawa, play on the white sands of its beaches. A place where distributors can gaze out over the deep blue skies and the shimmering ocean waters. A place where they can restore energy and revitalize health: which, after all, is the ultimate objective of the kangen water business.

Ohshiro is truly committed to seeing all of his distributors, wherever they might be in the world, realize physical health and complete peace of mind. In truth, the resort is expensive for Ohshiro to run, but it was conceived to benefit the distributors; Ohshiro's ideas are always directed far beyond what others see. One day, perhaps this particular idea—a golf course for his distributors—will come to the States.

Ohshiro has always seen the island of his birth as a window opening on the world, a platform from which to launch a global journey.

5. Once an Okinawan, Always an Okinawan

Ohshiro's ethos always seems to be moving in between the simple village man, who learnt the spirit of cooperation, humility and kindness in the hamlet where he grew up, and the businessman playing out a global drama on an international stage. The ethos fostered within him when he was a young boy continues to exert influence on him today, a grown man with a business mind. That same ethos is strong enough to form a platform, upon which people can start to build up new elements they have absorbed from the environment.

Still, Ohshiro is and always will be an *Uchinanchu*. The word means a native of Okinawa, but has implications of bumpkin, or rube. Historically, the word has even been used discriminatorily. When Ohshiro was at junior high and high school, it was strictly forbidden to speak in the Okinawan dialect; all students were expected to speak the standard Japanese dialect.

Today, however, the word *Uchinanchu* is slowly being reclaimed and to take on a positive nuance. For their part, the *Uchinanchu* are generally considered to be "good, compassionate people".

Ohshiro, the unchanging Okinawan

By now, I have lived in the States for longer than I lived in Okinawa, but I always ensure to maintain my connections with the island which is my home. And while, of course, I have interactions with many Okinawans, I have never seen anyone who embodies the spirit of being an *Uchinanchu* as much as Ohshiro. He is an *Uchinanchu* through and through. Because he has such a deep love for *Uchina*, Okinawa. It is very unusual for someone, for whom global management is such a prominent part of their lives, to maintain their identity as an *Uchinanchu* so determinedly. Or, rather, to make so much of that identity, to proudly show it off to the rest of the world.

Ohshiro is an *Uchinanchu*, inside and outside. You can even tell from his build and his facial features that he's "definitely from Okinawa". He often speaks in Okinawa dialect, too. When I met him a dozen or so years ago, I had forgotten most of the old Okinawan dialect, but once I started to work with him, it began to come back to me. When you hear your old dialect, and begin to speak it yourself, you are filled with a strange, strong sense of nostalgia. It might not move you to tears, but the dialect of your home village is rich with the taste and times of old.

Ohshiro is deeply proud of his Okinawan roots.

In the past, Okinawans have suffered discriminatory treatment due to their place of birth, and have experienced great psychological turmoil as well as facing the many problems associated with the continued American military presence on the islands. But times change; today, many mainland Japanese—the *Yamatonchu*—express desire to live on the beautiful islands of Okinawa. But Ohshiro's loyalty—not to his country but to his prefecture—is greater than most. He is determined to see that the tax payable on his business profits is used for the benefit of his prefecture. At the end of seminars in the States and Europe, he will often pull out his sanshin (a three-stringed Okinawan instrument) and play a kachashi folk tune, getting the distributors up from their seats and dancing in the aisles. I had never seen such a thing in all my long years living the States.

His message of greeting to the attendees of the June 2014 Global Convention also demonstrates just how staunchly Okinawan Ohshiro is:

Today is the beginning of another forty years.

Both Enagic and I were born and raised in Okinawa. We left this island, spreading our wings across the world, and today have grown into a global company, with 25 offices across 18 countries. On June 23, the day we celebrate exactly forty years since the birth of Enagic, we are holding a Global Convention with a thousand attendees right here, in Okinawa, where our roots lie. It is from here, from today, that a new forty years will begin, for me, for the company, and for all of you.

Filling free time with sanshin and song

One of Ohshiro's main interests outside work is playing golf. He is pretty good, too, according to his golf buddies, mostly because he's been playing so long. Still, I won't reveal his handicap. Okinawa has a growing reputation as an island of song and relaxation. It's certainly true that the energy from the sun warms your body the whole year round, and the beaches are among the most beautiful in the world. The islands are also filled with a spirit of friendliness—as the local saying goes, "brothers from the moment you meet". The islands have everything you might need to relax. And they are islands of song and dance, too. The Okinawan islands truly are islands of peace. It can almost seem as if the American military bases are somewhere else's problem. The military presence has always been an issue that has divided the islanders.

Ohshiro enjoys a drink, and he often accompanies his sake with a song or two on the sanshin, an instrument he can play with considerable skill. Playing the sanshin is a recreational pleasure for Ohshiro, but even professional players have commented on his talent for it. He has been singing since his boyhood and still today he has a good voice for it. He will often perform at seminars in the States and in the EU. Perhaps it's his unrelenting love for Okinawa. People of all colors get up and dance to the sound of his sanshin; there is a distinct pleasure in watching them all moving their bodies in time with the music. The music from a sanshin from a tiny island in the Pacific rippling out across the global stage, tangling everyone up in dance. What could the power of the music be? The spirit of a man who truly loves Okinawa is here, too, coursing through each note.

Ohshiro has composed an Enagic company song, entitled Flower of 'happiness with health and longevity'. The song takes the form of a ryuka, the poetry of the Okinawa islands. The song imposes new lyrics over an existing melody, and it is this song that Ohshiro sings at conventions and seminars around the world.

Flower of 'happiness with health and longevity'

1. LeveLuk was born from Enagic
   Kangen Water was born from LeveLuk
   Hundred and twenty years of life
   by drinking Kangen Water
   Let's make the flower of compassion bloom

2. In order to achieve true health
   Hundred and twenty years of life
   By spreading the message of compassion
   to every one
   Let's make the flower of heart in bloom
3. If 50s and 60s are buds beginning to flower
   Then the 70s and 80s are flowers in bloom
   Your life becomes hundred and twenty years
   Let's make the flower of happiness
   with health and longevity bloom

It is often said that *Uchinanchu* are very conscious of their Okinawan origins. People say it's because the sound of the *sanshin* runs through their veins. It is certainly true that there is something special about the sound of the *sanshin*, something that plucks at the heartstrings. Perhaps it is because that sound hints at the painful history of the once-stricken islands. Once, when I visited Tokyo, a dozen or so years ago now, an old friend invited me to join him at a restaurant in Shinjuku. After dinner, he dragged me to a karaoke bar specializing in Okinawan songs. Since I don't really sing karaoke, I ended up listening to his renditions of *ryuka*. His version of *Futami Jowa*, a popular folk song, touched me deeply. He was an elite civil servant in the finance ministry, living in Tokyo, but he often came to this bar, perhaps because

the sound of the Okinawan *sanshin* still played in his heart. Today, he is back in Okinawa, having retired from his government post and taken up an executive role in a local bank. There is nothing quite like the *sanshin* of Okinawa.

Ohshiro has always loved the *sanshin*, ever since boyhood. Perhaps he hears the pain, the mistakes, the setbacks, the emotion, the sorrow and the joy of those times in each note that he plucks; perhaps they all come flooding back as he plays. This power of the sanshin has been a great support to him. Wherever he might be overseas, be it in the States, Canada, France, or Asia, the sound of Ohshiro's *sanshin* rings out, bringing with it the scent of the old island. One, I saw him perform on the *sanshin* with some distributors improvising on their guitars, together with another playing the konghou, a type of Chinese harp. It was the musical equivalent of an Okinawan *chanpuru*, a dish which throws all types of ingredients together. It was a unique combination, but they soon harmonized into *Amazing Grace*. There was nothing strange about the way it sounded.

People in Japan consider the simple, everyday food of Okinawa to be extremely healthy: *tofu chanpuru and goya chanpuru* are currently particularly well-renowned. These dishes have made their way across ocean waters; first to Tokyo, and now even as far as Los Angeles. Ohshiro's musical chanpuru has also left the island, to be met with the rapturous applause of our distributors. I am cheering him on, too: *Come you, you Uchinanchu, you can do it!*

Riding in tandem around the world

Ohshiro's identity is strongly defined by his wife, Yaeko. They have known each other since elementary school. Yaeko is from the same village, and went to the same school—although Yaeko, younger than Ohshiro by six or seven years, was in a different year. There was a time when Yaeko thought of Ohshiro as a big brother-type. They are happily married, a real pair of lovebirds. Since he first expanded the company into the United States in 2003, Ohshiro has made the trip across the Pacific dozens of times. He's also flown to Europe and all across Asia, but Yaeko is always by his side. She does work as his secretary, but it's more than that; they are bound tightly together as husband and wife. It seems no exaggeration to say that without Yaeko's tireless support from the inside, her husband would not have reached the same heights of success.

This episode occurred during a flight from Tokyo to Los Angeles. Ohshiro had decided to travel first class. First class seats are different to business class seats, and the seats were arranged so that the seats were vertically parallel. This is to give each traveler the maximum possible level of privacy. But it also means that without standing up on his seat, Ohshiro couldn't very easily talk to Yaeko about the business to be conducted on the coming trip. They never flew first class again. What a shame! Unless Yaeko is quite literally by his side, he can't get on with his work. It's a story that's testament to just how important she is.

Ohshiro's instinctively gusty personality means that things are always very direct with him. Sometimes he'll yell out orders to staff, sometimes it will go further: "How many times do I have to tell you before you get it? Just get out!" He never means it, though. It is Yaeko, with her kindness and concern, who will placate the bewildered staff.

These lovebirds also create a good impression on distributors. In recent years, the divorce rate is high in both the States and Japan. The model of a couple loving each and helping each other for thirty, forty, fifty or more years is gradually disappearing. Enagic's core corporate principles aren't just focused on physical health; realizing mental health is a core principle, too. And so the model of marriage embodied by Ohshiro and Yaeko is testament to what can be achieved if those principles are followed.

The two of them travel through life together, as if they were peddling forward on a tandem bicycle. And it is Yaeko who is controlling the pace. At dinner, they will both order something different, then share it together, quite happily.

Yaeko's role is fundamental; she is Ohshiro's secret to success

A partnership as perfect as a ring

"Change your water, don't change your wife".

This is one of Ohshiro's oldest jokes, one he often pulls out at seminars. I'm never quite sure whether the American couples at his seminars are applauding his joke (since the divorce rate in the US is so high) or whether they are applauding his perfect English. Either way, he appreciates the applause. For this saying encapsulated the model of his marriage with Yaeko.

Ohshiro sees it as his mission to improve people's health, and this can be done by switching from tap water and bottled water to kangen water. Bottled water does not have a comparable alkali concentration to kangen water, which gives it only limited capacity to restore the natural acidity of bodies which have become overly acidic. Neutralizing our acidified bodies also has an antioxidative effect. Ohshiro calls out the same thing at every seminar: "Change your water to kangen water! It's the first step to health!". And then: "But don't change your wife!". The first half of his rallying cry is about business, but the second half is about morals, the ethics of marriage. This is important. Modern society is becoming increasingly superficial when it comes to love: marriages are like contracts, they last for a certain time and then both parties up and say goodbye. So perhaps it's not right to treat his heartfelt words—"don't change your wife"— as nothing more than a joke. The breakdown of families, in Japan and in the United States, is caused by problems between the husband and wife. So all the advice we can take, we should use for our own benefit.

After that tangent, let me return to my main point: that Ohshiro and his wife Yaeko are seen by many distributors as a model couple. Sometimes, Yaeko is invited to attend seminars as a speaker and she is very good

at it, too. It may well be the case that have a woman lead the discussion at women-only gatherings is more effective. The same goes for talking about what's happening inside the body, and the beneficial effects on ailments which only impact women, too.

You could describe the relationship between Ohshiro and Yaeko as the relationship between diamond and gold. Together, diamond and gold make a single ring. The highlight of any wedding ceremony is when the bride and groom exchange rings as symbols of their becoming joined together as one; the groom pushing the ring gently onto the bride's finger, the bride doing the same for the groom. Today, these rings are expensively made and set with diamonds. But in the past, rings were simple twists of wire with the slightest of decoration. Surely there can have been few wedding ceremonies in which rings were not exchanged.

It's easy not to notice, but the glittering diamond is supported by a base of gold. Gold is beautiful, does not rust, feels luxurious. And it has just the right amount of luster to perfectly complement the brilliance of diamond. The Ohshiros are a couple in tandem, a partnership, and it is Yaeko who takes on the role of the golden band, the base of the ring. Without this base, the ring will not work as a ring, no matter how opulent its jewels. Without this base, the ring is not a ring. If the base is not sturdy, the diamond will wobble; who knows when or where it might fall. The diamond can sit safely only when the gold setting grips it firmly. Only then can it show off its shine. The gold band rests quietly under the diamond, modest about its presence.

The beauty of teamwork is that the team members can perform their own roles as instructed by the leader, while celebrating their own sacrifice. The team will voluntarily push themselves down to push the leader up. When those at the bottom start to make trouble, the leader will be overshadowed. The supporting act should shadow the main act, should guide the spotlight onto the star. That is the very definition of "supporting". The same can perhaps be said for this husband and wife. They certainly embody these roles when it comes to work. Sometimes, however, it is Yaeko who appears to shine like a diamond, but perhaps that is just because I am biased.

As Ohshiro often says, "Change your water, don't change your wife".

This principle of working together like the parts of a ring applies to the internal workings of a company, too. It is a good way for a boss to work with his or her team. Indeed, from 2013 onwards, the company sales slogan has reflected this perfectly: "Let's Unify".

Success isn't just for the special

Following Ohshiro's story of success, it becomes clear that success does not only come to people who are somehow special. Anyone can be a success. The only condition that needs to be met is persistence: the light of success will never shine on you if you give up in the face of failure, allow yourself to drown in it. Once you have slipped underneath the surface of the water, everything becomes negative and proactive ideas are starved of the oxygen they need to thrive. Suffering, failure, setbacks. You have to change your perspective and see them as steps on the way to success.

This is a lovely story that gives one strength.

Once there was a man who raised a donkey for many years. Over time, the donkey became ever frailer; it was losing the vitality it once had. The man decided to get rid of the donkey, but no-one would take it and he could not bring himself to kill it. After a lot of thought, the man threw the donkey into an old, dried-up well in his back garden. Every day, he threw dirt into the well on top of the donkey, intending to suffocate him. Perhaps he thought it would be kinder on the donkey. Every morning and every evening, he used a large shovel to throw dirt down the well. The donkey felt the dirt showering down on his head. The dirt showers continued for weeks. Each day, the donkey would shake the dirt off from his back and onto the ground, then trample it down with his four hooves. And so the ground on which the donkey was standing was raised, little by little, day by day, by the dirt that the man was throwing down the well. In the end, once enough dirt had been thrown down, the donkey was able to escape from the well.

Donkeys are often mocked for being silly and slow, but this donkey's idea was very clever indeed.

In life, people have to contend with all sorts of troubled raining down on them from above: suffering, unexpected trials, sadness. But there is not a single person in this world who has never gone down a difficult path in life. It's the way of the world. But each person has to make a choice: whether to decide the suffering and the pain is too much to bear and instead to complain and criticize, or whether to turn around and battle with your ill fortune head on. There can be no victory without battle. And if you lose, the worst that can happen is you're back where you started. When you're up against a wall, the best way to fight yourself free is with defiance. Don't simply sit in the well and give up hope. As long as you want to get out of the well, as long as you want to see the light once again, you will find a way.

It may sound a little rude, but I don't believe that Ohshiro has any superhuman powers, or anything more special than the average person. He is completely and resolutely ordinary. Some of his staff might think that President Ohshiro is a genius, but he is just like everybody else in this book. What he does have is an outstanding knack for survival, an unshakeable spirit, and the ability to accept a storm of troubles as an inevitable inconvenience, to face them head on, and to turn them into elements for success. Success isn't a present that only special people can receive. It is something given to people who want it and who work for it. Even if you're from a tiny island, even if you're from a poor family, your dreams of global success can still come true. That's what Ohshiro is telling us.

A few days ago, I watched a DVD of a Japan Broadcasting Corporation (NHK) production, borrowed from a friend, on Otomo Sorin, a sixteenth century feudal lord who converted to Christianity. One quote, attributed to him, struck me deeply: "Defeat and suffering are trials we must bear, but we should not think of them as misfortune. Just as gold is burnished in the flames of the fire, so do such trials raise us up to better humans".

From tiny streams to a great river

Being careful with your words is no different to being careful about how you live your life. When words are chosen cautiously and considered carefully, those words can become someone's motivation, their energy. I cannot forget the phrase that cropped up during my conversation with my old teacher, Unten, and his wife. A phrase that sums up Ohshiro's beginnings and his place in life now. He started out from a poor family, a small village, a tiny island. What he describes, collectively, as his "origins". These origins were all seemingly so insignificant. Alongside these disadvantageous origins came unfavorable conditions, difficulties, failures, then survival and eventually resurgence.

It's easy to take a negative approach and think of these beginnings as having been minus points for Ohshiro. But if we look at the big picture, albeit in hindsight, these small beginnings are like tiny streams, or rather, the energy of tiny streams. Each individual stream may not amount to much, but put them together and the energy of each stream converges into a great river.

The Amazon and the Mississippi are great rivers only because of the many tiny streams that flow into them. There can be no great river without first a tiny stream. Once a river has become great, it must create tributaries if it is to sustain its might. The workings of nature almost appear to be an expression of how we live our lives. The business world, too, is a reflection of our way of life.

It's okay to be small. There's no reward at the starting line. We can only expect to receive our reward once we have run for the goal, battled all the way to the finishing line.

Unten's wife had it right: it's a principle that has always applied and always will apply, across the entire world. Ohshiro takes this principle and makes it a reality in business. He has carved out tributaries from Okinawa to Tokyo, on to Los Angeles, then to New York, then all around Asia. Today, those tributaries flow into a great river, which courses around the globe. New tributaries continue to flow into his river of success, now from South America and Russia.

Yes, I've done it, so you can too!

Chapter Two:

A Character-driven Company

Organizations are alive. Just as people breathe, laugh, cry, and feel sorrow, so too organizations are filled with hope and despair. It's no surprise, since organizations are run by living, breathing humans. The phrase "corporate culture" was something of a buzzword at one time, and it's certainly true that each corporation has its own unique accumulation of culture, traditions, and history. Even companies working in the same industry—high tech, for example—will develop different corporate cultures, reflecting the differences in top management and ownership. In a way, corporate culture is like the shadows cast by the owners over their companies. That's why the culture at Apple is different to that at Hewlett Packard, which is different in turn to corporate culture at IBM. These differences and the cultures in which they are reflected work to create strong corporate identities, which unite employees and becoming the driving force needed to meet the company's goals.

Culture can't be built up overnight. But Ohshiro is a charismatic figure. His personality is reflected very directly in his management, and it moves very quickly through the business conducted at Enagic. That's the mark of Ohshiro's corporate DNA.

Business is Speed

The remarkable accomplishments of the past twelve years are testament to Ohshiro's character. The company has grown at an extraordinary speed. One Korean businessman I know has an interesting theory. According to him, a person's approach to work is a reflection of their national character. What comes next is interesting. Koreans will dig the earth with their hands, he says, while Japanese will use a shovel. Americans, on the other hand, will bring in a bulldozer to do the job. Hands, shovel, machinery. It's not just the amount of work or the scale of work achievable that changes. It also makes a big difference in terms of whether your goals are short term or longer term. If you bring in a bulldozer, it means you've got to already be fixated on a point way past the horizon. But if you're digging with your hands or with a shovel, the only thing you're looking at is the hole in front of you. The size of the job ahead will also make a difference to the type of tool you need to use.

Ohshiro's character means he can sometimes be somewhat brusque. Almost like a bulldozer. Except he's already halfway across the field before you've even got the engine on. It can be hard to keep up. "Do it first, think about it later", he'll command. Of course, it's not possible to do everything with just a bulldozer, especially not work that requires delicacy. That's why you also need shovels and hands. So instead of standing around sluggishly, pondering and wondering, you should get up, get to it, get to work. And if you end up being wrong, you can fix it as you go, finding solutions and innovations to get back on the right path. That's Ohshiro's philosophy. It's easy to understand, too, if you look back at how he has lived and how he has grown his business. He spent a good many years working in accounting, but in terms of character he's a born salesman. He's always thinking one or two steps ahead of his staff, so if they don't catch what he's doing they can end up being left for dust. He's always got the pedal to the floor, which means that sometimes he can whip up a lot of dust and dirt in his wake. There's also the adverse effect of too much speed. So sometimes, alternatives have to be suggested and changes—lots of changes—have to be made. But the fact that Ohshiro is known as a man who "gets things done" is thanks to his ability to adapt to the situation in hand. There are pluses and minuses about his way of doing things, but what's certain is that his "speed management" has brought him a great deal of success so far. I'll talk about this more in Chapter 3: Creative Business Sense, Creative Business Strategy.

Gutsy Decisions, Quick Decisions

Back when we were learning about theories of management, we were taught that the decision-making processes of management should be drawn out for as long as possible. The reason being that if you take enough time, new information would come in, which would allow the decision-making capacity of the management team to gain traction. Perhaps this style of thinking doesn't cut it anymore in today's world of super-fast, high-tech information exchange. Ohshiro's philosophy, as I've already mentioned, is to "move forward, even if you're mistaken". In other words, don't delay and just get on with it. Once you've done it, then you can start thinking about whether it was the right thing to do or not.

His rapid decision-making really is a sight to behold. During a business discussion ideas can fly out of him, one after another. Ideas which he then grabs hold of, shapes, and immediately puts into action. He'll sometimes have staff start making calls straight away to put things to bed. His staff always have to be prepared for his bolts out of the blue; they never know when he might declare, "I'm transferring you to New York tomorrow". It's not unusual for him to make big decisions on the spot: "Right, next month, we're opening our new branch!" But he's mostly directly on target; which is doubtless why he was able to get the company this far having started with nothing. It's this kind of decision-making that has made it possible for Enagic to move into markets in the United States, the EU, and Asia in such a short time.

Incidentally, there's another story about national character that's relevant here. Italians, it is said, act before they think. Germans, on the other hand, think before they act. And Japanese? We think and think and still don't act. If this is the case, then Ohshiro must be an Italian. Because the Japanese tend to be overly cautious, to the extent that we miss the opportunity completely. Perhaps it's because of the Japanese culture of nemawashi, the process of slowly building to a consensus decision by gathering support from co-workers through an informal process of consultation.

Unwavering Endurance

As I mentioned in the previous chapter, Ohshiro more than once seriously considered shutting down the Hong Kong branch. But nothing could shift his conviction that the Hong Kong branch could be the gateway to the Chinese conference, the foot in the door to the Asian market. Hong Kong also offered a number of benefits in terms of its geographical conditions and business environment. So he could not give the order to shut the Hong Kong branch down. He was unwavering, he endured, and he invested for the future. A dozen or so years ago, Enagic had tried to open a branch on the Chinese continent. After a great deal of time and a great deal of money, permission to open a branch was refused. It had been a bitter experience. Most people don't want to make the same mistake or go through the same unpleasant experience twice, and so they curl up their tails the run and hide. One well known management principle is: "if you can't avoid loss then mitigate it". But that theory holds no water with Ohshiro.

This reminds me that although we opened our Mexico branch four or five years ago, the business has yet to bud, let alone blossom. Some people in the company are pushing for the branch to be closed once the current lease is up. But Ohshiro shows no signs of wavering.

If he had taken a short-term approach and shut the Hong Kong branch, would we still have achieved the same penetration into Asia we've managed today? Today, it's the Asian block that leads the entire global group and it seems likely that this trend will only continue and the gap widen. Business for Enagic has only just started in Asia; I'm looking forward to seeing where we'll be opening branches next.

And perhaps in a few more years, the Mexico branch will be our foot in the door to the entire Central and South American market, much as Hong Kong is now in Asia.

If you're going to work with Ohshiro, you have to be ready for the challenges intrinsic to his out-of-this-world ideas.

Ohshiro the Risk Taker

Ohshiro isn't afraid of mistakes. Perhaps it's because of everything he's had to endure in his past. If you become completely hardened to mistakes then you'll never make your way back up to the surface, but if you can use your mistakes to take you to the next level, then they can be an asset. Ohshiro is a risk taker; it's part of what he calls his "science of setbacks". But if you're a risk averter, your fear of failure stands in the way of your drive to move forward. Put a delicious dish in front of a risk averter and their first instinct will be to question whether there's any chance it's rotting.

But failure is part and parcel of business; risk is always involved, too. Running the Enagic Country Club certainly isn't risk-free, nor is buying up restaurants with real estate; there's no guarantee of success. There's an element of gambling involved. But everything will have been calculated clearly in Ohshiro's head, too. The restaurant that he bought had the potential to become a headache; but now, five years later, it's comfortably on a trajectory to success. The Country Club may have, in the future, a synergistic effect on the main business, of water ionizer sales, as well as local turmeric sales.

Ohshiro is a risk taker when it comes to his staff, too. He'll pick up people who've made mistakes, who've been rejected by others, and give them responsibility. Some people live up to expectations; other don't. But Ohshiro's all about putting them on the job and seeing what they can do. After all, everyone knows it's harder to stop once you've started and reached that certain point of no return. It makes sense to take risks.

As the saying goes, "you can't catch a tiger cub without entering a tiger's lair". But Ohshiro takes it a little further; he's a true risk taker, getting right inside the lair and stroking the adult tigers while he pockets their baby. It's not because he has either physical or fiscal strength. It's just his character, his programming, something that all successful people share: no fear.

Eleven years ago, we held a seminar is Las Vegas. Afterwards, Ohshiro headed off with Yaeko to one of the casinos. I don't know how much he bet but I know he won big, around ten thousand dollars. Some of the other staff, who'd made nothing but losses, were heard to mutter "I guess money just made more money". But what they didn't know then is that Ohshiro immediately set it all aside to be shared out among the rest of the staff on the trip.

The only place to find a tiger cub is in a tiger's lair. Taking the risk-free route means walking the long way to success. The fact is that millionaires will have failed more times than those with nothing to their name.

Workforce Motivation: Theory X

In the 1960s, Douglas McGregor was a professor teaching at MIT Sloan School of Management in Boston. During this period, he published research on theories of human motivation, dubbing them

Theory X and Theory Y. These theories were to have a significant impact on modern management studies. These classical approaches to management, Theory X and Theory Y, are based on the logic of dividing up management style into two polar opposites, A and B. The logic should then be adapted to each employee in order to see results.

Put simply, Theory X involves using punishment and reprimand to motivate employees and increase productivity. Theory Y, on the other hand, involves using back-patting and praise to increase productivity. So it's a question of whether you base management style on the carrot or the stick. Whether or not a manager follows Theory X or Theory Y will depend on how they see those working for them. Theory X-type management is based on the idea that employees are inherently lazy and will not motivate themselves to work, while the Theory Y approach considers employees of having the ambition to move forward and the ability to motivate themselves. In the first case, it certainly is true that if you leave a person with no self-motivation to their own devices, they won't get the job done. So the manager has to scold or to dish out some sort of punishment. But in the second case, the employee will get on with things him or herself, so there's no need to constantly give instructions or orders. In fact, with Theory Y-type employees, it best to keep managerial intervention at a minimum.

I think that today, in the States, many people are far too quick to praise their kids. The stick is still used with gusto within military organizations, of course, where the expectation is that all rules will be strictly followed. But in most cases, the trick lies in using both the carrot and the stick; that's what makes a good manager. The other point to remember is that Theory Y won't have any effect on some employees. Just as Theory X won't work on others. So a good manager needs both a carrot and a stick. Sometimes, a manager might appear all tough and Theory X-ish, brandishing their stick, while secretly being Theory Y on the inside. The way a person works as a manager doesn't necessarily reveal much about his or her personality.

Ohshiro's Generosity

Ohshiro doesn't have that particular fussiness that sometimes comes from being an islander. Instead, he's filled with a spirit of adventure, itching to sail away across the great open seas. So he's not interested in low-level failures or losses. Clashes with staff can often be caused by this difference in approach. The staff have a tendency to make their decisions based on units of thousands, tens of thousands. But Ohshiro thinks about things in terms of hundreds of millions. It's a characters shared by Ohshiro and many other successful people. Rather than wasting time and energy on the details, they think about the bigger picture and concentrate their energy on that.

This anecdote remains from Japanese history. Hideyoshi Toyotomi, who unified Japan and ended a long period of civil war in the sixteenth century, was particularly fond of his bird, described as a Tancho crane. Having a pet was, like having a hobby, a good way to relieve street. One day, the retainer responsible for looking after his crane accidently let it fly away. He came before Hideyoshi, convinced that he would be sentenced to die for his mistake. But Hideyoshi just laughed: "There's nothing to worry about, the whole country belongs to me". It was as if the bird had just escaped into his back garden. People who can't think of the whole of Japan (or of their own country) as belonging to them won't understand this way of thinking. Ohshiro is a man with a big heart, happy to welcome back former staff, people who have failed over and over. Not everyone in the company will always agree with his decisions. Nor is it the case that everything he does contributes to further success; sometimes things do backfire.

An Animalistic Sense of Smell

As humans, our sense of smell is much weaker than that of a dog. In turn, an elephant has a much more powerful sense of smell than a dog. They use the ends of those long trunks to sniff the grass and leaves, determining what can be eaten and what can't. Apparently, the soles of the feet at the end of their tree-trunk legs are equipped with sensory receptors so sensitive they can feel the vibrations through the ground caused by the movement of other animals. What's more, an elephant is somehow able to detect lightning from up to 25 miles away.

Ohshiro has an animal-like sense of smell. In a meeting about organizational restructuring, or a staff re-shuffle, or a promotional campaign, he'll soon be coming up with idea after idea, despite not having made any preparation. This ability isn't down to experience, it's more to do with his outstanding capacity to "smell out" the right managerial approach. His ideas are instantaneous and unexpected, so it's not the case that everything always goes well. But he's perfectly capable of conducting a seminar for over an hour, in front of anywhere between 500 to 1,200 distributors, with no speech prepared, no notes, and sometimes even a sudden change in topic. He's able to move forward, sniffing the scent of the audience, allowing his sense of smell to guide him in the right direction. Ohshiro's management and direction are also strongly influenced by this instinctive sense of smell.

Two Thousand Dollars of Compassion

Ohshiro can sometimes speak critically, but he is overflowing with compassion. His compassion of heart was something he was taught to have by his mother. This same compassion spreads throughout his distributors. There was a time when a new distributor was in a lot of trouble. She came to pick Ohshiro up at the airport; much was discussed during the car journey. Ohshiro realized she was in financial difficulty, so he gave her a token of appreciation for picking him up. It was a four figure sum. She went on to work harder than most to establish a strong foundation for the opening of the Washington State branch.

A man of Filipino descent had become a distributor. He said that he had experience of working for a Japanese multi-level marketing company. But he was on the brink of financial collapse. He had started selling kangen water machines, but had not yet found his stride. Even the twenty dollar check he wrote as payment for promotional products bounced. If it had been a mistake in calculations, that might have been understandable; but it seemed that he had become an Enagic distributor as a result of extreme financial pressure.

Ohshiro realized the strain he was under, and decided, out of compassion, to pay him two thousand dollars a month for three months. He rented an office in New Jersey and focused on sales on the east coast. Today, he makes a great contribution to the company as one of the top distributors in the country. A man whose twenty dollar check once bounced is now one of our millionaires. Helping others will lead to being helped yourself.

For the New York office, Ohshiro chose an office building in the middle of Manhattan, where rents are sky-high. New York is the financial center of the States—and of the world. Compared to Los Angeles, New York is a world city. It's also close to the EU market. Success in New York created a bridge linking the east coast to the EU market, and raised the Enagic Group up onto the international level. If we look back over the history of the New York branch, we can call the branch as it stands today the fruit of Ohshiro's compassion.

No Ax Swinging

Ever since the establishment of Enagic, it's been almost unheard of for Ohshiro to let anyone go. Staff whose productivity is low are not fired; instead they might be placed in a new section where they can learn a new role. He wants to see people find a better fit within the company before feeling forced to let them go. Staff who have been moved within the company need to scrutinize themselves and their performance. They need to think about why they have been moved to their new section. Moving staff around regularly does cause some breakdowns in communication, but it also allows staff to become familiar with multiple roles, which means gaps can be filled should they appear.

It was a few years ago. The company was trying to streamline labor costs and other associated costs. Streamlining labor costs helps to lower incidental expenses; it kills two birds with one stone. When Ohshiro was briefed about how the company could streamline, he immediately cut down any suggestion of reducing labor costs: "We don't need to do any of that. Just focus on sales". There aren't many companies which pay 100% of health insurance costs, even among big companies. It's well known on the inside that cutting even just half of those costs would mean huge savings every year.

I recall another episode. The attendees at a managerial-level meeting had been discussing how to cut expenditures. They came up with a few different proposals and submitted them to Ohshiro. One of the specific suggestions therein was a restructuring of company personnel. The entire team got an earful. "Before you start firing people, you should think about how to create new jobs. We've got nearly 200,000 distributors in the States. So why can't you create more jobs?".

It's true that it's easy to rearrange and restructure personnel. But the people getting fired have children and families to take care of. No everything should come from the top downwards; if lower-level staff can think creatively, then those ideas can realize market expansion without the need for cutting jobs.

The Mechanics of Reverse Psychology

Not firing staff. The years of bitter experience that Ohshiro endured are doubtless the source of this stance, a sympathetic one toward his staff. If talk turns to letting someone go, Ohshiro will immediately start imagining what a struggle that person's life would become after redundancy: "But he has a family, kids…" And he's not wrong. But his determination not to fire staff also aids the application of the mechanics of reverse psychology. When a person who knows that he should be scolded is instead shown sympathy, that person feels encouraged and happy. When a person who has failed at something is encouraged nevertheless, the normal reaction is to get back up and think: "I'm going to fix this!" On the other hand, if a person is simply shouted at for their failures, that person will wither in confidence, convinced of their own uselessness. The idea of reverse psychology is also important when disciplining children. Should parents scold their children when they are disobedient? Or should they bribe them with candy to be good? It's not possible to say which option is good or bad. The decision must be made based on the circumstances and the environment in hand.

Ohshiro is particularly good at employing reverse psychology. Recently, a certain department had been recording low productivity. Ohshiro changed up the staff, changed up the products, and even made alterations to the office layout. But productivity remained low. So Ohshiro turned his focus to one particular staff member. The staff member's colleagues were pretty surprised: what was it about this guy that made him so right for the job? Ohshiro's reverse psychology has started to work, but we'll have to wait a little longer for the full results.

Chanpuru Thinking

Ohshiro is a big fan on Okinawan food. For a start, it's healthy and low in calories. It's made with delicious ingredients, native to tropical islands, which are bursting with flavor. Fish, vegetables (many of which are air freighted from mainland Japan), *awamori* (an alcoholic drink native to Okinawa), sake. If his meal is accompanied by the sound of a *sanshin*, then he'll soon be grinning from ear to ear. Some of the most famous dishes from popular Okinawan cuisine are *chanpuru* dishes. *Chanpuru* means "mixed together", and dishes like *goya chanpuru* (made with *goya*, or bitter melon gourd) and tofu *chanpuru* can be made anywhere, anytime, by anyone. And they always taste good. *Chanpuru* is similar to the Korean dish *bibimbap.*

As you become familiar with the various aspects of Ohshiro's management style, it becomes clear that he takes a *chanpuru*-type approach. *Chanpuru* is a mixture of lots of different ingredients, balanced to ensure that it tastes great and to make sure that the most is made of each ingredient without allowing any one ingredient to drown out the others. So if you make *chanpuru* with tofu and bean sprouts, you have to make sure that the tofu doesn't lose it distinctive taste while still complementing and enhancing the taste of the bean sprouts. And the bean sprouts have to do the same for the tofu. Otherwise, the dish will only taste of one thing, and the whole point of making a *chanpuru* is lost. We can say the same for *chanpuru* made with goya and tofu. One of the most important things about making a good *chanpuru* is using ingredients which are dissimilar to one another.

Ohshiro often mixes up his staff, in *chanpuru*-style reshuffles. It's his attempt to get the best possible performance out of every single member of staff. But he has to repeat his *chanpuru* reshuffles often because the staff aren't performing as well as they might. So it's an iterative process, but one with a deliberate objective. Some staff don't like and complain, of course.

He also takes a *chanpuru* approach to marketing. The idea of commission *chanpuru* was a good one too, linking together commission from the sales of *kangen* water machines with commission from turmeric sales. The decision immediately encouraged a greater focus on turmeric sales. *Chanpuru* used to be thought of as something cheap that you could make with just leftovers. But as interest in the dishes of Okinawa has grown, it is now seen as healthy and delicious. It seems that if we change the way we look at things, the way we feel about them changes, too.

Crouch Down for a Penny

This is something that happened recently. I was chatting with Ohshiro as the two of us faced each other in a hotel restaurant. I can barely remember what we were talking about, but it was something to do with work. Ohshiro doesn't really make small talk. It was evening and the restaurant, empty, was quiet and calm. We finished our discussion, then stood up and headed for the exit. Suddenly, Ohshiro crouched down and picked up a single penny that had been dropped on the floor. "Pennies are important", he said, and passed it to one of our companions. He took one more step forward, then crouched down again to pick something up. "This isn't a penny", he said, and stood up.

I felt like I had witnessed something significant in this behavior. Ohshiro certainly lives a simple life, even now, but as he crouched down for the penny I got the sense that, subconsciously, he was always aware of the terrible struggles he went through earlier in life. Ohshiro acts big, treats distributors and staff to good dinners. There's nothing cheap about him, but he has known the bitter experience of a life so poor that even a single penny catches your attention. He went through failure after failure, of not knowing how to deal with each day, each coming day; a succession of struggles. "Take care of the penny", as it is said. Be grateful for even a single penny, just as Ohshiro is today.

It is as he always says: "Our company is for people in need" and "Make sure you pay commission quickly". It's true that the company takes such policy seriously. When people experience hardship, they often feel the urge to force that hardship onto somewhere else, someone else. In our hearts, there is the desire to make other people's poverty and hardship into our own profit and happiness. It we could all be passionate enough to not wish our hardships upon others, the world would be a more peaceful, richer, and happier place.

Second Chances

Ohshiro often speaks of Enagic as "a company for the weak" and orders us to "find distributors from among the less well off and ethnic minorities". He himself was born and raised in poor beginnings. People who have experienced hardship can well understand the emotional state of people who are struggling. There are people within the company who make the same mistakes over and over, who find themselves unable to resolve problems. There are people who make the decision to resign, and others who have resigned from the pressure. But then there are also people who, having resigned, ask if they can come back and try again; they ask for a second chance.

Sometimes other staff and distributors don't like it, but Ohshiro will give anyone a second chance.

Make back twice what you lost before, he'll say, and put them in a new position. Of course, you can't base management on humanitarianism alone, so Ohshiro is well aware of the potential merits of giving these people their jobs back. And he adjusts things to make sure those merits will be realized. Ohshiro doesn't rely on a management philosophy that is defined by rules and regulations. It's a philosophy which allows him to react and adapt to circumstance. But that doesn't simply mean choosing between one option and the other.

Strategy Dinners

Ohshiro is clear: "Our company is does not take a standard approach, we have an unusual-way-of-thinking". His management philosophy is not based on everyday thinking. It's a flexible approach, one which is tailored according to goals and objectives. There are plenty of points which highlight this. Ohshiro's strategy dinners, for example. These are informal platforms, not bound by convention, in which the participants can feel free and relaxed. There's plenty to eat, plenty to drink. But it's at this same dinner table where we find ourselves discussing important matters, inter-office moves, staff reshuffles. I'm fascinated by Ohshiro's ability to pull it off. I don't think it's thanks to the good food, but these meetings tend to go as smoothly as the sake being enjoyed by everyone attending. Although that's not always the case. Sometimes, when we haven't been able to solve issues with the business, or make the improvements we should, or meet the targets that were set, the diners are treated to thunderous rebukes, causing a loss of appetite and the sort of indigestion felt when sake goes down the wrong way. Dessert at these dinners is not always sweet. But once everything has been taken on board, the strategy dinners will always end on a positive note.

Ohshiro also holds strategy dinners with his top group of distributors. Most of the top distributors are not Japanese, but they mostly love Japanese food, with sushi and sashimi a particular favorite. Of course, Japanese food is available globally now. At these distributor dinners, they talk mostly— unsurprisingly—about sales and sales promotion. The dinners are in held in English, and this platform for communication has allowed Ohshiro to improve his English considerably. His public speaking in English still requires a little work, but for someone who has never learnt English to fluency, he does pretty well with the food, drink, and conversation at these dinners. Wherever Ohshiro goes, he'll profess that awamori, an Okinawan distilled spirit made from rice, is the best choice of alcohol there is. The staff know about this and will prepare two bottles for him: one of kangen water and one of his favorite *awamori.*

Seating Plans for Dinner

Ohshiro cares a great deal about the table and the arrangement of the chairs for his dinner meetings. Because these aren't just ordinary dinners. For department managerial meetings, he decides who sits where according to the themes to be discussed. He absolutely doesn't sit people in order of seniority. Who sits at the head of the table will depend on what is to be discussed. And whether it's a round table or a square one, the person who is ultimately responsible for the project being discussed will sit directly opposite to Ohshiro. Often, of course, there is more than just one project manager. If it's a sales meeting, a number of key staff, including the sales managers, sit in front of Ohshiro. Non-core staff and executives will be sat to the sides if they are not directly related to the discussion topic at hand. This sort of seating arrangement helps to enhance good communication.

This pattern works whether it's a dinner meeting or a meeting in the office. Staff need to be aware of it too; it doesn't matter if you're a top executive, either. If you take a top seat when you're not needed there, you'll probably be asked to move. Put simply, people are arranged so that the people ultimately responsible for the task being discussed can understand what is required of them completely and take action accordingly. Once people have sat in a seat before, they tend to want to stick to the same seat. But that sort of thinking doesn't work with Ohshiro.

Stormy Starts at Morning Meetings

Every month, the whole company holds a morning meeting, where each department presents major upcoming plans as well as results from the previous month. It is an opportunity for inter-departmental cooperative play. Global reports take up much of the time available. Normally, Ohshiro isn't in attendance, but when he is there is a noticeable tension among the staff. He will talk passionately to the staff about targets met, raising morale, service, and global competition.

At one morning meeting, Ohshiro was irritated

at what he perceived as a lack of morale among the staff, and reprimanded them loudly. "The Japanese among you, in particular, why have you even left Japan to come here to the States? Don't you have any dreams? You have to work hard to fulfill your dreams! If you don't, there's no point in you being here in the States. All of you should just quit now". Some of the staff listening were extremely affected by his words. Sometimes Ohshiro does that: he gets angry at meetings and demands that people resign from the company, but that's not what he really means. The next day he'll be back in the office, full of candor, looking refreshing, ready to talk. These changes can often mean confusion for the staff.

But these morning meetings function well. Departments like country sales support, warehousing, and service take up a lot of space and have large offices. It's not the case that staff see each other every day. Thirty minutes in the morning isn't a long time, but it is an opportunity for staff to see each other, albeit briefly, and to get a feel for what is happening in other departments.

Everything Starts in Okinawa

Wherever Ohshiro goes, wherever he visits on business, whichever overseas office he works out of, Ohshiro always goes back home to Okinawa. It's not that he has nowhere to live outside of Okinawa. Materially speaking, he could "go home" to wherever he wanted. But the idea of "from Okinawa to the world" is seared into his mind. So if he's going back anywhere, it has to be Okinawa. It's where the Enagic business started out and it's where Ohshiro build up the foundations for his success today. It's where the teachings of his mother in his formative years were learned, it's where he dreamt his first dreams as a young boy, and it's where he made those dreams come true. Okinawa is the origin of Ohshiro, and the origin of Global Enagic, too.

We can even put it like this. Without Okinawa, Ohshiro would not be where or how he is now. Or, rather, Ohshiro strongly believes that it was the climate and culture of Okinawa that built him up to what he is today. It has long been said that Okinawans have a long life expectancy. The weather and the diet are wonderful for health. The people are not flashy, they live simply, as if nature were inviting them to. The fact that Okinawans pay close attention to their health may well be the reason why, today, Ohshiro works in the health and wellbeing industry. So, you see, everything did indeed start in Okinawa.

Failure: the Nago Global Center

In the spring of 2012, Ohshiro suddenly announced that the company would be "building an Enagic Global Center in Nago". A property was acquired and significant investment made to start up the center. But the idea was to end in complete disaster. Some staff had furrowed their brows on hearing the idea, but if they voiced concern it would be impossible to back down. Ohshiro already had blueprints for the plan and for the operation. He bought an old hotel and set it up with an international office, accountants, and a call center. The call center was linked to the Los Angeles call center and a 24-hour shift system put in place in keeping with Enagic's global approach to business. Nago is located near to Ohshiro's precious golf course, which made it convenient. The plan was that the baseball team staff (introduced in a following chapter), the golf academy staff, and distributors visiting from overseas could all stay at there.

But the plan went up in smoke. What Ohshiro hadn't seen was that Nago is a still a small town, of just 50,000 people. However wonderful a center he might built, there just weren't enough people to work in it. It was a significant miscalculation. In this high-tech, internet age, young people are drawn to big cities; the dream to work in the city is common to all ages and cultures. For islanders, in particular, the pull of the big city is still very strong.

Perhaps the Nago Global Center was inspired by his idea that "everything starts in Okinawa". Or maybe it was a desire to show some compassion to the island where he was born and raised.

Either way, operation was promptly cancelled and today, instead, a Global Center has been established in Naha, the capital. The fact that his beloved hometown of Okinawa is now able to meet the needs of distributors around the world is indication enough that "everything starts in Okinawa".

A Thrifty Lifestyle

President Ohshiro and his wife are proud of their simple lifestyle. That simplicity goes for their personal life, but for work, too, they don't drive around in a flashy car. And as long as Ohshiro knows where he is going, he will drive himself. Their personal appearances are simple and modest, too. Perhaps this modesty is a result of the hardship they experienced. They do not dress up, even for the biggest seminars; their simple elegance remains the same.

Industry leaders of Ohshiro's type are generally expected to be flamboyant, accompanied by fanfare, always in festival mood. Ohshiro's not like that at all.

He is an anomaly, an exception. He is more concerned about appearing to be one of the people than about appearing Presidential. Among the distributors there are people who have built themselves back up from severe financial hardship. And there are new distributors, too, who are still in the process of that recovery. Ohshiro is a role model for these distributors, and a role model for those that have found success, too.

We often hear about people who fail to plan: who can earn $500,000 or $700,000 in commission but still can't pay their taxes. So even while their earnings increase, they are incapable of managing their finances, chasing after material things, neglecting to save or put money aside for retirement. He is a role model against this kind of live-in-the-moment lifestyle, too. In this industry, distributors often move from company to company, always in search of greater income. That has the adverse effect of meaning that their source of income never stabilizes.

Ohshiro's unembellished, natural appearance and his simple, modest lifestyle strike a chord with many of the top distributors.

Overflowing Energy

Ohshiro is so full of energy it's hard to believe he's as old as he is. He doesn't let tiredness show.

Everyone, once they hit forty, will experience their body slowing down. It does depend from person to person, but once you hit sixty, many people retire, experience serious illness, spend long periods in hospital, or even need home-based care. But Ohshiro is still bounding with energy and jetting around the world. Okinawa to Hong Kong, Hong Kong to Tokyo, Tokyo to Los Angeles, then across to New York on the east coast, then down to Florida, and onwards to other states. Or perhaps Okinawa to Tokyo, then London, the somewhere in Germany, then across the Atlantic to New York, then onwards to Los Angeles. These are considerable distances. LA to Tokyo is a twelve hour flight, followed by a few hours in transit, then a flight to Okinawa that arrives after 10pm. Once he's left Naha, he has to go back to Naha. This is the sort of schedule that Ohshiro regularly follows; keeping up requires plenty of energy and physical strength, too.

On arrival in LA, Ohshiro is met by a member of Enagic staff who takes him straight from the airport to his office in the company building, where he will first review documentation. On the day of arrival, despite having just come from a long flight, he never once complains of being tired. He normally stays in LA for around a week, during which time he will hold North America managerial meetings, meetings with top distributors, and inspections of each department.

There are no rest days in his schedule. In the evenings, he will have dinner with distributors and staff, before heading home after 9 or 10 in the evening. These dinners aren't just for entertainment; they are business meetings. None of us know where Ohshiro gets the energy to keep up with this tough schedule: some staff conclude, jokingly, that he must be some kind of monster. Ohshiro will tell you that it is because he has been drinking kangen water for thirty years. His own body is proof of its effects—and should not be forgotten as a PR tool. It's simply not possible to do as much work as Ohshiro does without taking in plenty of energy. Somewhere, somehow, he must have a secret as to how he burns his energy so efficiently.

Whenever he is in LA, the one thing Ohshiro can't miss out on is playing golf with his staff. He's been playing golf for a long time and is one of the ways he revitalizes himself. After work, it's perhaps what he most loves doing. The fact that he invested his own money in a golf course near his home village and even set up a golf academy to teach local young people how to play golf is perhaps enough of a hint to just how passionate he is about his golf. He only plays as much as his work allows, but his passion for golf springs from his ability to still see himself as a young man. We can achieve youth in both mental and physical aspects.

As for Ohshiro, his lifestyle and good health are surely thanks to the tiny island of health consciousness where he was born.

Fukutsukan: House of Perseverance

This story took place in October 2014, when the weather in Okinawa was still beautifully warm. A typhoon was unfortunately edging closer, but we decided to take an early morning walk. We left the hotel and headed toward the harbor. The town was tranquil, yet to awaken. There was not a sound to be heard, not even the bark of a dog. The strong storm winds beat against the trees lined up through the town, creating a sense of unease, but still we battled onwards, enjoying our first walk in Okinawa for a long time. We walked onward, toward the ocean side. We passed what looked like an elementary school to our left, then walked through a large residential area. The main street was beginning to come alive with taxis and commuter cars. We headed toward that main street, then turned left. In front of us was a white building, resembling a private residence, with a placard on the front: Fukutsukan, or House of Perseverance. We wondered what it could be, then passed on by. But as soon as it was behind us, it started to niggle me. So when we passed a gas station,

I asked one of the employees: "What's that building back there, the one called Fukutsukan?" But the employee didn't know either. That didn't stop us; we decided to head back to the building and find out. For some reason, my curiosity had been piqued.

A person on the street at last had an answer: "it's a museum commemorating Kamejiro Senaga". There's no-one in my generation who hasn't heard of Senaga. Now dead, Senaga was a politician and member of the Japanese Communist Party, who shook the very foundations of politics in Okinawa. Until 1972, when Okinawa was returned to the sovereignty of Japan, the islands were under the control of the United States Civilian Administration. Senaga was one of the men who fought against the civilian administration, boldly calling for the return of the islands to Japanese sovereignty, under the banner "Yankees Go Home!". When we were still kids, we found Senaga and his fearless spirit intimidating. Back then, Communist Party members were subject to ruthless crackdowns and Senaga spent many years in and out of jail. Once Okinawa was returned to Japan, Senaga served as a member of the House of Representatives, and continued to be a unique figure in Okinawan politics. Whether or not you agree with his political ideology, his fighting spirit is something we can all aspire to show in our own lives.

When I saw the Fukutsukan, I immediately and intuitively linked it to Ohshiro's failures and struggles. Ohshiro managed to sneak through three near-death experiences then face up to continued hardship, while still continuing to head toward the goals he had set himself. Just as his "science of setbacks" shows, he took a life of adversity and learned enough to turn it around. Realizing your dreams is not something you can do with perseverance, unwavering endurance, and fighting spirit.

In one corner of the old elementary school that both Ohshiro and I attended there is now an Enagic Museum. It tells the story of Ohshiro's thorny path to success. It is well worth a visit. It is good to learn from history, to project the history of another onto our current selves. Whatever our age, we should always strive to learn and to better ourselves by learning from others.

Life as Water

"Change your water, change your life". It's Enagic's trade mark. If you change your water to kangen water, your whole life will change too. This slogan is a concentration of all the aspects of Enagic's corporate philosophy I have introduced so far: realization of physical health, of financial health, of mental health. If your body is not healthy, life will be difficult. If life is difficult, you will find yourself becoming depressed. This is why everyone should try kangen water as it is so beneficial to health. The fundamental principle of good healthcare management is drinking good quality water. Day-to-day, we don't think about the water and the air. That's because we don't have to; they are there for us whenever and wherever we need them. If we look at the providence of the universe and of nature, everything that humans need to survive is, in principle, free. How strange it is that we do not need to pay a thing for any of them.

It seems apt to introduce the "Six Teachings of Water". In Ohshiro's Presidential Office there is a hanging scroll, on which the teachings are written. It was a gift, but presents a highly accurate observation of the properties of water. It also appears to advocate that we try to live our lives much like water.

1. Water gives vitality to all living creatures
2. Water flows ever onwards, seeking out its own path
3. Water has the courage to overcome whatever obstacles lie in its path, but can allow take the shape of the vessel which contains it
4. Water is inherently pure and can wash away the impurities of others; it accepts both

the good and the bad

5. Water becomes force and becomes light, performing endless tasks in production and in daily life, without asking for any reward

6. Water fills the oceans, evaporates into vapor and clouds, falls as rain, changes into snow, and transforms into mist, yet never loses its own true nature

Chapter Three:

Creative Business Sense, Creative Business Strategy

In this chapter, I will talk about Ohshiro's unique business ideas and senses, as I have seen them from the sidelines. Business people need to have creative qualities, otherwise they will find it very difficult to come out on top in the competitive business world. They can't rely on examples, either. Ohshiro's management philosophy and his business strategy are creative. By this I mean that they are unique, unparalleled. Although now successful, Ohshiro has developed his own "science of setbacks", an approach that can now give comfort and courage to many people, filling them with incentive and driving them forward.

1. Ohshiro-ism

a. Ohshiro-ism: five kangen principles

"Ism" refers to a distinctive system or philosophy, as is capitalism or communism. It can be added to a name to refer to that person's philosophy and the guidelines by which they live their life. Companies can have "isms", too, helms which steer them in certain directions. Without a helm, a ship cannot journey across the sea; it cannot tell which direction and it will stall at sea. The world of business is like trying to grip the helm of a ship sailing across a stormy sea.

It has been nearly fifty years since Ohshiro left school. The first twenty years were a succession of hardship and failure. At times, things got so tough that he thought he wanted to die. Over the next twenty five years, he built up a foundation for a successful domestic business, achieved exponential growth, then expanded into a global brand. This success was helmed by Ohshiro's "Five kangen"-ism. Kangen, incidentally, means to "return to the origins", or to "return things to how they should be".

Each of the five kangen principles has elements which overlap, but they can be summarized as follows.

i. Return to health

Our dietary habits have become dominated by a tendency to eat whatever we feel like at the time. So we eat instant foods, which are convenient if nothing else. As a result, although food is meant to sustain us, ironically our eating habits can end up harming our health. The obesity rate in the States now stands at two in three adults, one in three children. The food that people are choosing to eat and the volumes in which they eat it are inhibiting good health. Few people actively control their diets, while keeping in mind an image of themselves in good health in the future. Improving health, returning to our once healthy bodies: this is an important idea to advocate. When we are born, our bodies are the embodiment of good health; we must try our utmost to return to that state.

ii. Retuning good, fair rewards

To work is noble; it is the responsibility of the company to remunerate its staff in recognition of that work. Enagic has in place a commission system that enables its distributors to be rewarded with adequate income. The eight point business model, discussed later, is a model for attaining high levels of income.

iii. A quick return in real time

Remuneration should be paid quickly. At Enagic,

payments are not bundled into a single sum nor only paid at the end of each month. Instead, multiple payments are made. This is because the distributors don't only conduct sales once a month, but multiple times throughout each month. So Enagic pays distributors in real time, as and when they make sales.

iv. Returning thanks, returning compassion

Enagic is able to survive thanks to its distributors. So the company must treat its distributors with gratitude and with compassion. The company must also show the same gratitude to its staff. When people interact with each other with compassion, those feelings are reciprocated and the impact is enhanced.

v. Returning to the local community

Companies have social responsibilities. It is only right that the corporate earnings should be returned to the local community. Companies should maintain contact and communication with the local community and should contribute to enhancing community welfare, particularly in respect to young people.

These five points are Ohshiro's "ism", his core philosophy. He is constantly encouraging staff to always strive to put these points into practice, so the philosophy can be achieved in real terms.

b. Management philosophy

Management philosophy at Enagic is consolidated into three principles of health:

1. Physical health
2. Financial health
3. Mental health

These three principles are like a trinity; they cannot be divided from one another. If the body is healthy, we can do any kind of work, which will bring us financial rewards. And if we are blessed with both health and economic prosperity, then a weight is taken off our minds and we can achieve peace of mind. The inclusion of mental and spiritual elements in this philosophy is a direct result of what Ohshiro has experienced in his life.

More than 60% of the adult human body is water; for babies it is around 70%. Without water, we cannot live, and in order to maintain our health we need to drink good quality water. The reason that one big company after another is launching bottled water products onto the market is because the health and wellbeing industry is booming. But there are big differences in quality between bottled water and kangen water.

Ohshiro's philosophy is that by selling kangen

water through a networking system, he will be able to provide compensation plans that allow distributors to maximize revenue, thereby allowing the company to pay them greater revenue than other MLM companies. It's a plan to ensure that distributors can achieve the best possible financial health.

Mental health—peace of mind—isn't something you can buy with money or objects. But many people suffer because of financial reasons—they get divorced, they are in pain. There is a correlation between one's financial position and health. It is common knowledge that our finances can build up our lifestyles but they can also be the cause of our downfall. The key to Enagic's success has been to implement, unfalteringly, this trinity of corporate principles.

c. Spreading compassion

Ohshiro always emphasized how we should be compassionate to one another. I have already talked about how his mother's teachings still reside in his heart. This is why he is so dedicated about spreading the word about *kangen* water, the secret to health, good news that he wants everyone to know about. Of course, some people will dismiss his message as nothing more than business talk and PR. There's not much we can do about that. But in truth, you can't really understand Ohshiro's mindset without first understanding his *Uchinanchu* spirit.

There is a phrase in the Okinawan dialect, *chimugurisan*, which means to have compassion for others. Literally, it means to have "pain in the heart". In other words, seeing the pain and the sadness of another causes you to feel pain in your own heart. *Chimu* originally meant "heart". Your heart would ache with compassion. There are other similar phrases in Japanese, such as *kimottama ga ookii*, "to be fearless", or "to have a big heart".

There is another word, *yuimaaru*. It does not have the exact same meaning as *chimugurisan*, rather it is one rank above it. This word means to "help each other". In the past, if a village suffered damage from a typhoon—a collapsed roof or a blown down fence— everyone in the village would go from house to house, helping to repair and mend each property in turn. Their "hearts would ache" for their fellow villages, which is why they would *yuimaaru*, help each other. Today, that same spirit exists, although it now manifests itself differently.

Ichare bacho de. This saying "brothers from the moment you meet". It is another indication of the oceanic and open spirit of Okinawa. If you introduce yourself to someone you're meeting for the first time as "an Uchinanchu", then their hearts will open to you; you'll find they tell you things not normally told. It's strange but wonderful. Sometimes, Japanese people can behave strangely. They might avert their gaze upon seeing another Japanese person in the lobby or elevator of their vacation hotel. But they will greet people who appear to be Korean or Chinese. I've experienced this myself. The Uchinanchu are surprisingly shy, but once they know you're also from Okinawa, you'll be fast friends in no time.

I've already written about how Ohshiro is an Uchinanchu through and through. The period in which he was raised and grew into adulthood was one when the Uchina spirit was particularly strong. So it's easy to understand why he is so committed to this principle of spreading compassion. Within this principle are remnants of the pain he felt as he battled poverty as well as the hope and compassion that inspire his desire to see everyone—even the poorest among us— achieve success. Ohshiro often says how we should "help the less fortunate through our business". It is through this manifestation of kindness that Ohshiro hopes to see distributors find success for themselves and—his true intention—to see them helping others.

d. The three factors of success

Just as people set goals in their own private

lives, so companies, too, must have clear objectives. As long as companies set management principles and a corporation vision, honor those rules that should be honored, target their energy and focus on implementation and operation, they should be able to find success. Ohshiro's success, simply stated, has been the product of the following three factors:

1. Good products: We are often told that Enagic products are expensive, but we are very seldom told that they are poor quality. And while they may be expensive, many people still buy them. There will be expensive and cheap options for any given product. It's all about how you opt to market them. Think about cars; our products are Mercedes Benz and Lexus class. We don't align ourselves with the cheaper products on the market. The high class of our products is without doubt, as the many testimonies to its effectiveness prove.

The fact that Water Quality Association USA awarded a quality accreditation to our world-first Enagic products is also testament to the quality of what we offer.

I would like to add my own personal comment here. I had injections for allergies for over twelve years, seeing a specialist doctor once a week. Once I had been drinking kangen water for three months, I decided to skip an appointment to see how my body would react. I have never again gone to see the allergist who treated me for those twelve years. Drinking kangen water has also enabled me to cut down the numbers of hours I need to sleep by 1.5 hours a night. It's thanks to the fact that the molecules of kangen water carry nutrition right to the very extremities of my veins, as well as help to make the digestive process more efficient. This means that energy is burned up much quicker than when drinking ordinary water. Even now, past seventy, I feel fighting fit, with plenty of energy even on just five and a half hours of sleep.

2. Eight point system compensation: The eight point system of commission in place at Enagic is unique in enabling distributors the opportunity to make significant levels of revenue. Ohshiro is extremely proud of this compensation system. This system is the result of hours of thinking and countless revisions. It is just as many distributors themselves demonstrate. Enagic products stand out among our competitors as much higher in quality, but if we do not ensure adequate return to our distributors, then they will perceive no advantage in being part of our business. The products and the commission paid for them must be in tandem to ensure success.

3. Creative marketing: marketing strategy is the key to communicating your products and your

commission system as attractively as possible. There is no-one more skilled than Ohshiro in this field. Talents managers come up with new ideas for promotions, incentives, and awards all the time, but none of them can produce ideas to compete with Ohshiro's. Of course, I can't go into too much detail, since it's an element intrinsically linked to strategy and corporate secrets.

In short, though, products, profit, and marketing form the three strands of a strong braid, or the three legs of a sturdy tripod.

e. Blessed with the right people

To achieve success, every business needs to be blessed with the right people. Seitoku Takara is an accountant who has been associated with Enagic for 35 years now. He has 45 years of experience working as an accountant for many companies, and over that time has held been asked for advice about personnel countless times. He has seen the rise and fall of many companies. "What do you think is the key to Ohshiro's success?", I asked him. The answer came back without hesitation: "He has good people around him".

I felt somewhat taken aback. Ohshiro can talk tough and be short. He'll say what he thinks without holding back, as is often the case with Okinawans. He's been in business for a long time now, so he's well aware—just as we all are—of how to convey his message without words. He's the sort of man who says what he thinks, so staff who are nervous or lacking in confidence will wither under his words. It was just as Takara said; it was true that Ohshiro was blessed with good staff.

I cast my mind around who works in the company HQ and in the branches. I thought about the faces that regularly surrounded Ohshiro. They were certainly all excellent staff. Many used to work in large companies, with a great deal of experience. How on earth had Ohshiro managed to recruit them? What had they perceived in Ohshiro, that had inspired them to leave the capital for the less glamorous option of Okinawa? Although Enagic is a global company now, it's still not in the big league with the multinationals. Perhaps for most people it wasn't about the company; it was about Ohshiro's quintessentially Okinawan honesty, his wandering samurai entrepreneurial spirit. They could see their future with him, inside him. Ohshiro has reaped an excellent harvest of experienced personnel, then sent them around the world to enhance company sales.

2. Enagic Business Systems

Ohshiro describes the business methods, approaches, and systems he uses in Enagic as "Enagic Business". The business adopts the network marketing approach, in which the sales channel sees products pass directly from the Enagic factory to the end consumer. To distinguish his business from other network marketing businesses and to reflect his unique creativity, Ohshiro uses the term "Enagic Business". The Enagic Business is made up of two fundamental systems: the marketing system and the zero system.

a. Marketing system

It's often said that humankind's greatest invention was the wheel. And one can only nod in admiration at this testament to the wisdom and innovation of our ancestors.

Did early humans just get fixated, one day, on the idea that "surely, there must be a quicker way to get home than just walking?" For hunter-gatherer humans, the question of speed, of whether one was fast or slow, could be, quite literally, a matter of life and death. And the wheel provided the answer. But once you have wheels, next you need something to fix them together. Which means you need tools. After all, a single wheel isn't much use. Before long, it seems that humans worked out how to get horses and cattle to pull carts, transport hunting hauls, and drag harvests back home. This isn't necessarily an academically robust description of the invention of the wheel, but the point is this: humans are smart, and being smart allows us to create systems. Once those systems are in place, they start to enable us to get even smarter.

One day last year, I got rid of my old computer and bought a new one instead. Even with my old computer, being able to use email had allowed me to work more efficiently than I ever had before. Things were so much more convenient—I could work whenever, wherever. But with this new model, when I open my mail it automatically pulls up a calendar listing all my appointments and to-dos. And so things are much the same today as they were long ago: we're smart enough to build systems, and these systems teach us how to develop new and better systems.

Ohshiro says that "business is systems". Each of these systems link together, overlap, and in doing so generate synergistic effects.

i. Why choose Multilevel Marketing as a sales channel?

Ohshiro's business philosophy is all about just how well he can link up his systems. If the systems are poorly linked up, at best, there will be no synergistic effect. At worst, the business will be adversely affected. Ohshiro has outstanding skills when it comes to sales. He will make adjustment after adjustment until the sale is closed.

In the 1980s, when kangen water ionizers first appeared on the market, every company opted for the in-store sales route. Large-scale sales companies and small companies alike chose the classic retail route.

When Ohshiro set up Enagic, he tried using this same retail route. He went around retailers, as if he were selling video players, and had them stock his ionizers on their shelves. But the products only moved slowly, and Ohshiro realized his company was once again at risk of failure. After considering all his options, he came to understand that the main problem with traditional retail was that the retail staff were recommending the products without understanding their effectiveness and impact. Further, they were unable to recommend a specific product from among those in their range. So Ohshiro began to think about how he could develop his own, unique networking business. He was convinced that a system centered on sales people who understood the effects of the product was the best possible option.

Enagic products are good products, with definite impact and functionality, but if you have never used one, you simply can't know how good they are.

Nobody can recommend with confidence something they haven't tried and tested for themselves. Ohshiro hit upon this basic marketing rule. If people who already knew how good the products are were put in charge of selling them, they would be able to recommend the products with confidence, which would put the buyer at ease, and lubricate the sales process. This concept was the starting point for the networking sales model that Enagic adopts today.

Ohshiro devoted himself to developing a payment system for this sales channel that would enable speedy payment; a commission system that would mean distributors could enjoy revenue unparalleled anywhere else in the industry. With his mind set on global expansion, he also reached the conclusion that he would need to be able to control the means of production in-house, too.

It goes without saying that, sometimes, sales companies are sometimes at the mercy of manufacturers. Even if sales are going well, if the manufacturer is unreliable and the supply unstable, then the sales company will not be able to meet stable demand. Sales companies with no control over manufacturers, then the situation is akin to expanding your businesses into a politically unstable country; you are constantly worried about what will happen next. Ohshiro bought a production plant from a certain large company at just the right time. Eventually, the scale of production stabilized to the point where Ohshiro was able to expand from domestic to international sales.

ii. The "distributor" brand name

In Japanese, Enagic customers are referred to as hanbaiten, which we translate as "distributors". Normally, "hanbaiten" would refer to a retailer or wholesaler. It may have been a term Ohshiro coined in reference to Sony's "dealers".

Once a person becomes a hanbaiten, that person is manager, owner, and president. The same nuance does not apply to the standard definition of "distributor" in English. Even if a distributor is the owner, status-wise they will never be president. It's about how the terminology is used. It was a little strange, at first, to hear the distributors referred to as "President Yoshida" or "President Abraham". But there's surely nobody who doesn't like being referred to as "President". Are people not more likely to push themselves, in order to meet the expectations associated with the title? This is the impact, the power of branding.

Even in everyday life, the way we choose to "brand" our words can be significant. For example, we could rebrand a direct criticism—"the way you do things is wrong—to something like "perhaps you could try a different approach?". The second option is attuned to the person to whom the comment is directed. With this option, they're less likely to become emotional; they might even take it as a positive comment. The second option, the "branded" approach, shows respect for the other person, and shows that you have realized that they are indeed trying (even if it's not going so well). Use a word like "wrong" and it will sound like a condemnation. Use a phrase like "try something new" and it becomes a suggestion that still acknowledges the efforts of the other person. And there is no-one who will not listen to simple suggestions.

In business, and in particular the one-on-one approach adopted by network marketing business, verbal branding is necessary too, especially when meeting face-to-face to talk shop. Unless we take care to use the right words, kind words, respectful words on a daily basis, we will not be able to apply the verbal branding we need to with the right speed and precision. Calling our distributors "Presidents" makes sure they are branded in the best possible way they can be.

iii. The eight point system

The eight point system is the source of Ohshiro's "magic power". Some have even called it genius. It's a system of compensation that nobody else has managed to replicate. It is someone hard to explain in this limited space, but in short it is a completely unique commission system, unlike anything else in the industry. The standard commission model is known as a Binary plan; this is where the distributor recruits "downline", in other words new distributors are subordinate to the enrolling distributor and pay commission to that distributors. We can refer to this as the "vertical axis".

In Ohshiro's eight point system, however, the vertical axis is limited to eight stages, after which the distributor has to expand their new distributors horizontally, because there will be no commission beyond that. This is called the "horizontal axis". So these "eight points" comprise the vertical downline and the horizontal downline. In order to maximize commission, the vertical axis should be extended eight stages and the horizontal axis as far as possible— the further it extends the higher the distributor's rank will become. With a Binary plan, the vertical axis can extend further down, but with Ohshiro's eight point system, the distributor can extend both the vertical and the horizontal axes, creating a balanced structure, and maximizing the commission they are paid.

Key to this system is the fairness of the commission itself. Network marketing systems can be misunderstood as pyramid schemes or similar, but the eight point system created by Ohshiro serves to undo that misunderstanding. His business systems, including the eight point system for commission, have been recognized as a trademarked business model by the government of Japan. It took five years for the trademark to be granted. It was the first such business model in this industry to gain this recognition, although I will not go into the details here.

Further details on the eight point system are available in Enagic corporate brochures and other related literature.

b. Zero concept, zero system

Ohshiro has a unique approach to business, but his concept of "zero system" stands out in particular. Zero here doesn't mean zero in the sense of absolutely nothing; it rather means "almost nothing". Normally, when starting a business, one needs to raise capital, to get a range of products ready to be sold. In the network marketing world, it is standard practice to have sales quotas in place. The reward for matching that target—the prized sales commission—is then paid at the end of the month, one month in arrears. Not at Enagic. They try to pay their sales agents on a daily basis. This non-intuitive policy is the result of Ohshiro's "zero concept".

i. Zero start-up capital

Almost no business can be launched without capital. Most networking businesses, however, do not require a great deal of start-up capital. What is required, however, is stock inventory and working capital to get thing moving. Enagic distributors don't need to have access to significant capital at first. They can start from zero. This system is one of the distinctive features of Enagic.

Ohshiro still remembers when he himself was struggling financially. He well understands how it feels to be poor. So he started with a general rule to pay commission on a daily basis. Some of our distributors were people who had gone bankrupt, who couldn't afford to buy a car, who couldn't pay their health insurance premiums, who were facing crisis. Today, many of those distributors have now found success and are in a position to help others. This is the effect of introducing a system requiring zero capital funds. Of course, many people started off with a loan from family or friends, or by using credit.

I have heard it said that the origin of network marketing businesses lies in the door-to-door selling of Bibles by Christian missionaries. Whether that's true or not, some of our distributors include pastors and churches. Churches are places where many people gather, and many of those believers will have economic needs. A church will already have a number of groups in place; the environment is well suited to the launch of a network marketing business. The pastor of a church which has just become involved in the business will find him or herself having to work two jobs. The financial situation of many new churches is precarious; often funds are not sufficient to adequately support pastors. So it is not uncommon for pastors to continue the work of the church while also holding down a job in a regular company in order to make ends meet. A network marketing business is an ideal way to plug these gaps. As long as a pastor can make time and manage that time, he or she should be able to run the business alongside their ministry. Indeed, there are pastors who are contributing to the church by working in just this way. There are even cases in which pastors have sent large donations to their home towns, as funds to build new churches there.

ii. An arsenal of one

Today, consumers like to have infinite choice from a diversified and complicated selection. There seem to be almost as many options as there are people. These subtle differences bring about diversity. Businesses can exploit this diversity of character by developing "tailor-made" products. Think about cars; the number of models on the market today is countless. The size of the car, the color, the horsepower, the automatic handling, the manual operation, all the other options. You can't just say you "bought a car" anymore. You have to be more specific.

In this age of diversity, Ohshiro arms himself with just one product. Having said that, it is not exactly a single product; his big guns are the kangen water machines and kangen turmeric. Among the various kangen water models, the most popular account for the majority of sales. There are also a couple of dozen promotional products. Distributors focus on the machines and the turmeric to expand their sales. It goes without saying that the less you have to memories about what the product is, how to use it, how to store it, and so on, the easier things are. Adding more and more products to a range means expending more and more energy on sales.

Animal trainers might put a lion or a leopard in a cage and then show off how well they can control their big cat. But if they make one mistake, they're cat food. There are three items that every animal trainer needs: a whip, a pistol, and a stool. The stool is the most important. When training the animals, the trainer leans back against the stool, then sits with his or her legs pointing towards the animal. The animal tries to focus on both the trainers' two legs and the two legs of the stool. It becomes lethargic, as if paralyzed, and therefore easier to tame. I'm not sure what animal psychology is at work here, but the lion or the leopard will then listen to the commands of its trainer.

The same principle can be seen in the application of a strategic decision to focus on a single product. It is easier to concentrate on marketing when the number of products is lower. But today consumer preferences change continuously, so we must not be shut off to the idea of new product development. The life of a kangen water machine today is around 10-15 years, and the quality is as good as any durable. This single product principle also has an impact on the zero inventory approach I outline below.

iii. Zero inventory, no sales quota

Having a zero inventory system is another marketing mechanism unique to Enagic. In principle, the company only sells one Kangen water machine to each distributor. In special circumstances, the company many sell more than one, but in general the policy is implemented without exception. Those distributors who wish to buy more than one might argue that "all they have to do is sell them". But Ohshiro rejects this, calling it too short-termist an approach. The policy is also a means of preventing unnecessary stockpiling, just for the sake of increasing commission. Many network marketing businesses require their distributors to meet sales quotes, which in turn mean that the distributors must build up stock inventories to cope. Those quotas might be monthly or annual. This means pressure, of course, and some distributors are plunged into crisis. Can this really be beneficial over the long-term, for either the distributor or the company?

The zero inventory policy works something like an air miles system. Some companies require you to use miles accrued within a certain period; others allow you to keep your miles indefinitely. It goes without saying that for the traveler, the second type of policy is more convenient. Ohshiro's idea of zero inventory and no sales quotas weren't thought up from the company's point of view; they are distributor-focused concepts. Having an unnecessarily large inventory results in "dumping" (offloading stock) and plays havoc with prices. But if there is no stockpiling, then the price can be controlled. So the policy is good for the company, too.

iv. The positives of on-the-day payments

Most MLM companies pay commission at the end of the month. So even if a distributor makes sales, he or she has to wait an entire month to see that income in their account. People who are just starting out in business and people who are facing financial pressure will find that month-long wait hard. It's a hardship that you can't understand unless you have experienced it. And Ohshiro has, over and over again. On-the-day payments have been born out of the struggles he has endured.

As soon as commission is generated and calculated, the company will make payment of that commission within a few days. Payments will be made day-in, day-out, to the same distributors as required. This means that sometimes, after a weekend or a long weekend, a distributor might awake to find a handful of checks in his or her mailbox. And if a distributor goes away on business or vacation, he or she might return to a fistful of checks. On-the-day payments help to scratch the itch of every distributor. The objective of the system is to bring the waiting time for payment down to as close as zero as possible.

Once, I was invited to a Christmas party being held by one of our top distributors. I was stunned to see the pile of checks piled on top of his desk. "How many do you have piled up here, don't you need the money in your account?", I wanted to ask.

I heard another story, this time about an encounter on a flight. One of Enagic's distributors was heading from Los Angeles to New York. A stranger sat down next to her. She pulled out a bundle of checks from her handbag and started to count them. The person next to her eyed the checks, appearing surprised at how many there were. The two of them started to talk and soon talk turned to her job: "What sort of work do you do?" By the time they had finished talking and the plane had landed, the person next to her had become a distributor. This is the power, the wisdom, the positive of on-the-day payment.

v. Network marketing businesses start with one

Ohshiro cherishes each distributor as if he or she were a precious jewel. It's true that the company couldn't survive without distributors. But there are some who complain that he treats his distributors a little too well. Not least because their remuneration is so generous. Many distributors are inactive; they are in hibernation. But Ohshiro still pays attention to those distributors whose contributions are small. His years of experience have taught him that network marketing businesses are built on respect for each individual, that once one individual is committed that same individual can go on to have a significant impact. After all, Enagic might be a global company, but it started out as just the two of them, Ohshiro and Yaeko. The fact that the total number of distributors has now reached 650,000 is testament to how Ohshiro has always treated each and every individual as important.

It was August 2014. Ohshiro took some children

from the Enagic Golf Academy, who were visiting from Okinawa, to a country club on the outskirts of Los Angeles. As the children played a tournament, Ohshiro waited, watched, supported. Another child had come from China and that child ended up winning the tournament. Ohshiro immediately went over to the child's father to congratulate him. Then he took a snapshot of himself with the tournament winner.

I was watching from a distance. Ohshiro took out a business card from his pocket and introduced himself properly. I thought to myself how Ohshiro really was a salesman through-and-through. And I recalled what he often said: "Network marketing businesses start with just one". Most people don't approach people they've never met before and ask to exchange business cards. Of course, Ohshiro had a reason to speak to the man in this case, but for most people the exchange would end with small talk. But his approach, his salesman mindset, are different to most people. There is an old saying: "always assume the worst of people". But that's not how people appear to Ohshiro. To him, everyone he meets is a potential distributor. All of our distributors and our staff should learn from Ohshiro's outstanding salesmanship.

vi. The zero debt doctrine

There are two things that Ohshiro hates. Banks

and lawyers. When I say "hate", I mean something more like "avoid at all costs". Money that has been borrowed must be repaid. In which case surely it is better not to borrow it in the first place. That's not to say we should never look to the banks for help. But Ohshiro only uses banks now for real estate loans.

This is the thinking behind the Enagic financing system. It's not an entirely new system of financing, but it is unusual to see this sort of financing system in this sort of industry. In-house financing does not work to constrain in-house cash management because it rather works to increase sales. There are plenty of people who can't obtain loans from banks and other financial institutions. Enagic financing can provide covering fire for such people. The system is also set up so that even if the funds loaned prove irretrievable, terms are set for short periods so the loss is limited. Ohshiro is rightfully proud of this fact: Enagic is not a company that has any problems with cash management.

c. Learning from the Great East Japan Earthquake

In 2014, I had the opportunity to visit some of the areas affected by the Great East Japan Earthquake in the Tohoku region of Japan; a friend showed me around. We left the parking lot of the airport where my friend had come to meet me. As my friend drove, he explained how the sea was off to the right. "Can you see that handful of pine trees over there?", he continued. "It's a beach, and there were lots of pine trees growing along it. But as you can see, now there are just a few. Before, the row of pines functioned as a windbreak, protecting the sand".

I wasn't particularly surprised, until he continued. "Many pine trees were uprooted in the tsunami, and the uprooted trees floated along the water, crashing into houses and buildings, destroying them. Cars, too, were pushed along by the water and smashed into homes and buildings". I had seen and heard a great deal of information about the disaster, but this was the first time I had heard anything about this.

What does this desolation tell us? That things which are essential to our daily lives can, in times of emergency, become the very things which destroy us. This is the truth. Ohshiro hates loans; as a result he introduced a new system of financing into Enagic. Take out a loan and you can obtain the operating capital you need to start planning for the expansion of your business. When business is good and capital is flowing effectively—and when the economy is doing well—then the impact of a loan can be significant. But there is nothing to guarantee that business will always go well. Business is endlessly fluid; it is vulnerable to internal and external changes alike. At times like this, debt has the opposite effect: it puts stress and strain on the business cash flow. During this sort of emergency, things would be fine if the bank reduced payments on your loan or gave you an extension of a few months. But no such banks exist. Instead, they demand repayment.

Just as the pine trees and cars were thrown against buildings, destroying them, by the power of the tsunami waters, so too can money owed to banks destroy a business from the inside out. Ohshiro knows this, from his days as a Sony dealer. He lost everything: his company, his assets, his home. All because of a loan. That which we can ordinarily use as a weapon may be turned against us, with destructive force, in times of need. This is something every business person needs to be aware of, always.

After staying for several days in the area, we left with tears and prayers for the region and its speedy recovery.

d. Ohshiro's "Science of Setbacks"

i. Success built by two

In this high tech age, success stories can mean building a vast fortune overnight. Many of these people have set up their own companies on their path to success. Others have made their money—and name—by playing the stock market or investing in real estate. To be successful, you need both capital in the form of ideas and you need to have experienced failure.

Ohshiro and his wife spend much of their early adult life struggling through a series of failures, setbacks, and doors closing in their faces. They set themselves down in a tiny room in the Shinagawa area of Tokyo, without a penny to their name, and eked out an existence. Their only capital was themselves. What did they learn from their failures? Endurance, hope, ingenuity, tireless effort. And how to gamble, too. These qualities and skills became the capital that would lead them to success.

"What does it mean to be rich?" is something that I'm often asked. My reply is always the same: that being rich means that you don't need to ask the price of something before you buy it. It takes a lot to get here: a path marred with twists and turns, sometimes narrow, sometimes treacherous.

Now, for Ohshiro, it meant travelling to dozens of countries around the world to expand the business of kangen water across the 650,000 distributors currently in those countries. In Okinawa he is involved in more projects than can be counted on his fingers and toes: golf courses, real estate investment, leisure facilities.

His success story had lead him to a position from which he owns and manages multiple businesses.

It is possible to identify a number of key points underpinning Ohshiro's success. The major influence of his mother's teachings. Taking the world as his stage while keeping one foot in Okinawa, the origin of everything. Much of what he does can be attributed to what he learned from his mother.

ii. Ohshiro's "Science of Setbacks"

As humans, if we neglect to learn we lapse into laziness. If we stop learning we revert to an animal-like state. This is my personal theory. We can learn much from our eyes and our ears. We can imitate the actions of those who have found success, learning from it, finding a quicker path to our own success. We can learn from the failures of others, realizing that we should avoid running down the same problematic path. In other words, as long as we have the desire to learn, failure can become an important manual for success. "If at first you don't succeed, try, try, and try again". So the saying goes, and it is true that even if we take tumble after tumble in life, we might find a diamond as we hit the ground.

Ohshiro sees mistakes and failures as a bounty. Within failure are the vestiges of the energy a person has expended on developing ideas, making plans, and putting things into operation. Failures also contain a wealth of time and of wisdom. This means we do not repeat the same process. We can also add the uniquely Japanese idea of kaizen, "continuous improvement". People who see failure as futile are the same people who cannot keep forward. By taking a positive attitude toward failure, that very failure can become the platform from which we launch ourselves toward the next level. We have to find value in failure. Ohshiro describes his biggest failure to date as the closure of Sigmac Japan. But he is quick to point out that this cruel setback has, in fact, been the source of any number of invaluable instructions.

I see difficulties as an opportunity for constitutional improvement. If you allow yourself to be defeated by difficulties, you will be inevitably setback. If you instead seek win out against your difficulties and to push past them, then you will foster a tough spirit, able to cope with the environment around you. In other words, we should make ourselves stronger through constitutional improvement. Once you have experienced difficulty, you can have compassion for others facing difficulties. If we go through life without coming up against failure and struggle, we will end up weak and feeble, as if we had been raised in a glass house. Salesmen and women need to have the drive and the fight to get back up after they have been knocked down. Look at a boxing match on TV, at the viciousness of the counterattack launched by the opponent who has been punched out, knocked down. It's a fight back charged with a renewed determination not to lose. Perhaps it's human instinct. People who are cautious and try to avoid failure and difficulties from the offset do not have the courage to face difficulty head-on once it does arrive. Struggle is prerequisite for constitutional improvement. We need to be aware of this from the outset.

Living with adversity: we all know that the environment is a powerful force, able to change the humans who live within it. We can refer once more to the ancient Chinese tale of "Mother Meng's Three Moves": move next to a school, and your child is more likely to buckle down to work; move next to a merchant and your child will develop a flair for business. Live on a small island and you might think small; your dreams end up small, too. Bring a child up in a household where the adults suffer from alcoholism or substance abuse and the likelihood of the child developing the same problems as the adults rises, or so statistics tell us. As it is said, people are mere animals in their environment.

Ohshiro says that we can change our environments. He encourages us not to give into them. There is no rule that says you cannot dream big just because you live on a small island. We must shape our own environments, instead of allowing our environments to shape us.

"Yes, I've done it, so you can too!"

We can take these words from Ohshiro as a challenge: you and I are the same, which is why you can do what I've done. Ohshiro started from zero. Sometimes, his start was even worse, from below zero. In a minus situation, having nothing becomes a plus. So people who find themselves with nothing should consider the situation a plus and drive forward with as much will as they can muster. Simply put, people should never give up their dreams, no matter what the circumstances; they must cling onto them until those dreams are realized. Dreams don't really come in different sizes. You cannot take the dream of

another for your own. But you can look to the dreams of others as models for your own. First, create your own dream and your own goal, and then devote all of your energy to them. Without a dream, you are like a ship without a compass, not knowing in which direction you are heading. You do not know what lies ahead. You do not even know where you are standing right now.

We are in the GPS (Global Positioning Satellite System) age. With GPS technology, we can even find a car after it has been stolen. To not know, then, where we are in life is truly sad indeed. We need GPS for our own lives. Holding onto our dreams is one of the most important things we can do in life.

"Dreams aren't for dreaming, they're for making come true", says Ohshiro. It's important not to just tidy this statement away as the talk of someone successful. Enthusiasm, drive, and a plan for how to make your dream come true are all vital.

Chasing your dream requires the energy to be constantly on the move. Many people chasing dreams end up giving up half-way along the journey. They can't keep up with their dreams. But their dreams are only their own; no-one else can chase them. Just as each of us must be responsible for our own health, so each of us much manage the realization of our own dreams.

We must establish objectives, draw up plans, carry them out, reflect on our performance, and at times correct our trajectory. We must have patience, we must unwavering commitment, we must have hope, we must have conviction. If we have all these, then we will be able to overcome failure and hardship.

We must not complain about the adversity we have experienced in the past. Ohshiro is a role model for us in this sense; he has much to teach us. And he has the same message for all of us:

"Yes, I've done it, so you can too!"

iii. Loyalty to Sony

I have already talked about all the things Ohshiro learnt through his failure as a Sony distributor. If you fall down, grab hold of something and pull yourself back up again. There is one more thing to add here: Ohshiro's loyalty to Sony. He has only praise for the company in his speeches and always chooses Sony products for his household electronics. If Sony made cars, Ohshiro would doubtless be driving one.

Loyalty must be accompanied by a trustworthy character. However much loyalty someone might swear to you, if that person is not trustworthy, the only thing awaiting you is trouble. If the person is trustworthy, they must also be loyal, otherwise your relationship will be short-lived only. Success in business needs trust and requires loyalty to superiors.

It reminds me of this story. The Standard Oil Company, which was broken up around 1910 under the Sherman Antitrust Act, employed a man called John Dustin Archibald; he was known for his battle cry of "$4 a barrel". When he travelled for business, he would register his name, adding "Standard Oil, $4 a barrel" underneath. News of this spread through the other employees and eventually reached the ears of the President. The President decided that he wanted to meet the young man who was so committed to his company and his job. Eventually, the two men came face to face. It was the beginning of a relationship that was to see them lead the Standard Oil Company to greatness together. Archibald loved the company so much, was so loyal, that he signed the company's name right next to his own—nobody had to tell him to do that. Loyalty without greed will eventually be recognized and rewarded. John Dustin Archibald was rewarded by John D. Rockefeller, owner and founder of the world's largest oil company at the time, with a new position as Vice President.

What does this lesson teach us? That loyalty is a direct route to success. There are those in the network marketing business who move between companies, floundering this way and that as if caught in a torrent. But can success in the network marketing business really be found if powered by impatience, self-interest, and short-sightedness? Better to take the time to choose one company, to love its products, and to be loyal to it. Surely this is the quickest way to realize your dreams.

iii. Internal strength, external reach

"Internal strength, external reach" is my own phrase. By this, I mean that one should be firm and settled within, while at the same time striving to extend one's reach ever further. The Old Testament tells us of a prophet, named Micah, who spoke of the future awaiting Israel:

> *The day for building your walls will come,*
> *the day for extending your boundaries*

What he meant by this was that although at the time Israel was under attack, its city walls being broken down, the time would come when those walls could be repaired and rebuilt, and the boundaries of the nation of Israel extended. This verse has much to teach: to businesses and to individuals. We must first be firm and steadfast within; only then can we begin to expand toward the outside. If we are not independent, we cannot grow. Companies, too, must have internal strength, otherwise they will never be able to widen their scope. For Japanese companies, this means first establishing a firm basis in Japan, and only then moving on to a neighboring country, then the rest of the world.

The globalization of Enagic has progressed exponentially. It is a trend that seems set to continue. Domestic management and global management have quite different dimensions. First, internal management frameworks have to be consolidated. Within the Asian block alone, there are different languages, cultures, religions, legal systems. The world is diverse and complex. This means that we need to show similar diversity in our responses.

As for our ever-expanding global management, this is not something that can be handled by one person alone, no matter how much experience that person has. It is nothing like managing a shop. There are limits to the extent to which Ohshiro, as just one man, can manage the globalization of Enagic, and its further expansion. To achieve further growth and greater success through continued globalization, managers will have to stand together with Ohshiro, supporting him from the left and right, facilitating the company's expansion. It goes without saying that the information gathered from our distributors around the world is a significant asset. As we devote our energy to the development of new markets, we must be careful not to close our eyes to our internal framework of management.

> Unite the company together;
> internal strength, external reach!

Peter Drucker says:

The best way to predict the future is to create it.

Chapter Four:

From Now, The Future

1. The Winds of Enagic

Twenty years ago, a year-long NHK historical drama, entitled *Dragon Spirit*, was broadcast here in LA. The drama received a lukewarm reception; it was a little too slow-paced, painting an overly peaceful picture of the Ryukyu Islands (which later became known as Okinawa), and there was little excitement. What sort of winds really blew across the Ryukyu Islands during that time and what were they blowing the islands toward? The series portrayed the Ryukyu Kingdom in the late sixteenth and seventeenth centuries, when it was controlled by the Satsuma Clan, which was based in Kyushu, on the southernmost main island of Japan. I still remember it to this day.

What sort of wind is Ohshiro trying to blow into

the future? I shall try to get down to the essence of this question, while enjoying the blast of those winds. Ohshiro is still committed to the success of his business, but he has begun to turn his attention to what is beyond. Enagic has started to focus on giving back ("returning") to the community, and the scale of these contributions are set to increase. It is the social responsibility of any entrepreneur to contribute to local society; this is the true entrepreneurial spirit.

Of course, there are inward flowing currents, too; there must be committed efforts as a company to push forward with the globalization of the Enagic business. Here, I would like to introduce a few future prospects: both those which have been announced publicly and my own private hopes for the company.

a. Outward flowing currents

i. Mizuho no Sato

In a town not so far from Ohshiro's family home, there is a care home for the elderly called Mizuho no Sato. We visited the home in the middle of the Okinawan summer, when the heat was bordering on oppressive. The home is a five story building, surrounded by lush green fields. We were taken inside—the air conditioning was working nicely—and shown around. Mizuho no Sato was set up several years ago and has room for 44 adults; it is a fairly small facility. It also provides a number of services: it is a registered special care home for the elderly, it takes in short term admissions for daily care, it provides care to outpatients, and it can also support elderly people who require care but still live in their own homes. The home employs 38 members of staff, including part-time staff. The ratio of staff to residents is not quite one-on-one, but it is getting there. There is significant demand in the local area for the sort of services that Mizuho no Sato provides; at present, there are around 200 people on the waiting list.

We were shown around parts of the facility and watched a number of the residents receiving care; the oldest was woman aged 103, the rest were all over 90 years old. The day care residents were all enjoying watching the television. The cost of Mizuho no Sato is relatively low and the need for such care services in the local community is high. But any and all such retirement homes share a common worry: the financial side of the operating. As a matter of urgency, Mizuho no Sato needs to be looking at how it can expand in the future and how to improve its current financial situation.

Ohshiro has been involved with Mizuho no Sato since March 2014, specifically in a role to improve its finances. First, he set up the Long Life Club, through which Enagic can provide support to the home. This is the first time the company has been involved in local contributions focused on the elderly.

As we left Mizuho no Sato, Ohshiro was reminded of what his mother had taught him: to always be kind to others. Perhaps the old ladies in the care home had reminded him of his own mother, who had sadly already passed away.

A few years ago, I was invited to spend a few days at Ohshiro's vacation home. Unusually for the area, it had gate security. It was a large, two-story building, richly furnished. The view from his home stretched out across luscious green rice fields, beyond which lay the tranquil Pacific Ocean. Ohshiro hardly ever makes use of this home. As we talked, he said something to surprise me: "I hardly ever use this house. Perhaps it could be used as a day care center for the elderly people in the village". I could hardly believe what I was hearing—turning his holiday home into a care home? I had caught a glimpse of Ohshiro's abiding love for his parents. It is not by mere coincidence that Enagic is now supporting Mizuho no Sato.

ii. Dreams for the young

The Enagic Baseball Team

Okinawa, the land of long life, is blessed with the

kind of favorable weather that allows you to practice and play sports all year round. Japan's favorite sport is baseball; everyone plays, even small children. In the past, every company used to have a baseball team and they would all play against each other in leagues, but recently the number of teams has dropped— there is only a handful in Okinawa now. These teams play in what is known as the corporate league, and in Okinawa there are only six teams, including Enagic. The teams members are officially company employees. The number of people who play baseball tends to be high as it is a popular sport. Having the Enagic team creates added value for employees and contributes to improving the reputation of the company. The reason that the number of corporate league teams has fallen is not due to a drop in the popularity of baseball, but rather it is a question of the budget required to maintain such teams.

Industrial team members work as company employees while also dedicating time to practice; in Enagic, mornings are for baseball and afternoons are for office work. All of the team members strive to improve their sporting skill while remaining dedicated to their work; there are even a few younger players who are dreaming of getting to the professional leagues. There are seven or eight official games a year; our performance so far has been "not bad", says

Coach Morinaga.

The Enagic Baseball Team was established in 2009, after a statement by Ohshiro at a press conference in October 2008: "I have been thinking, as someone born and bred in Okinawa, what I could do for my local community. The level of baseball played at elementary, junior high and high school here in Okinawa is among the best in the country, but those talented players have nowhere to go in Okinawa after graduation. I would like to offer baseball as a means of enabling the young people of this prefecture to hold onto their dreams".

Enagic Golf Academy

On the way to Ohshiro's family home, we dropped into the Enagic Country Club. It was my third visit; the golf course, now complete, was truly a sight to behold. The turf had taken root and the fresh green grass contrasted with the azure sky and the cobalt blue of the ocean waters. It was so beautiful that even non-golfers would want to come here, just for the view. From the stand, where people were constantly teeing off, we gazed at the brilliant green of the course, then made our way to the temporary club house. The groundbreaking ceremony for the permanent club house was held in February 2015; work commenced not long after.

Shinyu Kakazu, Director of the Golf Academy, came out to meet us. We had first met several months ago in LA and we began to talk about our previous meeting. But my focus was not so much on the conversation as on what has hanging behind the Director's desk. A calligraphy scroll with the Japanese character *kan* (感), written in powerful strokes. It was a masterful piece. But why had he chosen this particular character, which means emotion or feeling. I asked Director Kakazu. He began to explain, turning and gesturing at the scroll. In Japanese, words can be formed by combining two or more characters. With kan, any number of characters can follow to form many different terms. Add *dou* (動) for *kandou* (感動), meaning "to be impressed"; or *sha* (謝) for *kansha* (感謝), "gratitude"; add *geki* (激) for *kangeki* (感激), "to be inspired"; *fun* (奮) for *kanpun* (感奮), "moved and inspired"; or even *ou* (応) for *kanou* (感応), "sensitivity". You can also add characters before kan, for example *choku* (直) to make *chokkan* (直感), meaning "instinct", or *ban* (万) for *bankan* (万感) meaning "a flood of emotions". It is a character that can be combined to create a myriad of human thoughts and emotions.

Director Kakazu explained how it was important to nurture sensibility (*kansei*) in young golfers. I was impressed (*kanshin*) by his story and listened intently, nodding. Young people who hope to become professional golfers must be trained in how to foster the sensibility of a golfer; this is a critical skill that can be the difference between victory and defeat. They must also learn to be impressed by the play of other golfers, if they are to be able to learn from others. Young people today are often criticized as having forgotten how to say "thank you". So these young Enagic golfers also need to learn how to have gratitude (*kansha*) in their hearts at all times for those who care for them.

The world of sports is all about winning and losing, or getting the best possible score. But it all starts with education of the spirit. I got the sense that under the banner of this notion of kan, the instructors were trying to teach their young players how to be free with their ideas and how to create their own options.

In the temporary club house, I was impressed at how the young golfers were first being taught how to think like golfers. This temporary club

house will, eventually, be transformed into a grand and permanent structure. And some of the young golfers here, too, will have realized their dreams of playing as professionals in the country clubs of Japan and the United States. The young players here have considerable natural talent and there are strong expectations for their future. Some golfers from Okinawa—such as Ai Miyazato and Ayako Uehara— are already prominent on the international stage. Their dreams weren't just dreamt.

Bringing the Golf Academy to the States

Ohshiro has wagered a big dream on these young golfers. In August 2014, he invited 23 members of the Academy to come to Los Angeles. I spent a few days with the party; the children, all full of energy, were aged between 11 and 18 years old. Some of the mothers had come with their children and were looking after the group. Actually, they seemed to be having more fun than the kids themselves.

It was their first time to Los Angeles. It was to be a week during which they felt impressed and inspired. In the outskirts of Los Angeles, they took part in their very first junior tournament, with impressive results. The children also took part in a US-Japan friendly tournament. The little kids from Okinawa played against the big kids from the States, trying their best to communicate with their limited English skills. Watching them, I got a sense of their potential for growth and for hope.

There is a saying in Japan, "Let your darling child travel", which means something similar to "spare the rod and spoil the child". It is a truth that still holds to this today. Travelling reveals new worlds. Children who travel can see these new worlds with their own eyes and find new opponents to challenge in these new worlds. The world is there to be won; if you stay in your own village or your own country, you will be like the frog at the bottom of the well—ignorant of the world beyond your immediate surroundings. We need to breathe in fresh air, find new opponents to challenge, refine our skills, refine our sensibility, and learn—always learn. Experiencing new worlds when you are young can help to broaden the perspective you have on life and on the world. It can also help to elevate their ability to take up the challenges to be won in this world. I hope that many more US tours will be planned in the future.

(For further information on this golf tour, see the article in the international edition of the Okinawa Times, October 6, 2014.)

Showing Young People the Future

For the past few years, Ohshiro has dedicated much of his energy to bettering the futures of young people. It is a new idea, conceived along with the building and operation of the Enagic Country Club. He established a Golf Academy, with the intention to create positive opportunities for children in Japan, and Okinawa in particular, and built the Academy facility from scratch. He took over the lease of the building which had once housed his elementary school, and turned it into a work facility. Practice was to take place at his very own country club. He created an environment where children could learn both theory and practice. The Academy facility is in quiet part of a secluded area, so it is the ideal place for children to focus on their objectives and improve their skills. The cost of attendance is low and many children come from the mainland to attend.

Around 30 young golfers, all hoping to become professionals, are enrolled at the Academy. Of those, 23 had visited to the States on Ohshiro's invitation. Once more thing struck me when I visited Director Kakazu at the Academy. On return to Japan, the children had written essays reflecting on their experiences in the States. Each of the essays had been read, signed and dated by Ohshiro. Now, Ohshiro is an extremely busy man, who is constantly travelling around the world. I tried to imagine him reading each and every one of these essays. Until that point, I suppose I had imagined that the Golf Academy was just one of Ohshiro's side interests. But that assumption disappeared in a second. I realized that he was very serious about the Academy indeed. He was thinking about the future of these young people. Despite his unforgiving schedule, he was spending time, money, and energy on this; it was much more than a hobby or a distraction. I could almost feel the weight of his expectations for these young people.

Here, I would like to introduce the essay written by one of the participants, fourteen year old Haruki Miura. It is my hope, too, that these young people will continue to dream big and to spread their wings around the world.

At the end of our US Training

Firstly, I would like to thank President Ohshiro, without whom we could not have gone to the United States. I was able to realize that in order for us to spread our wings around the world, our perspective has to widen to take in the entire world. I hope to make the most of this experience by one day becoming active on the international stage.

I would also like to thank the parents and teachers who supported us during our time in the States, as well as Mr. Shiroma. Thanks to the support of the parents, I was able to have an injury-free, incident-free training experience, while the teachers enable me to play some good golf. Thanks to Mr. Shiroma and the other coordinators, our time in the States was enjoyable and went very smoothly.

I am grateful for many of the things that happened in the United States and intend to make the most of what I have experienced. I have decided that they best way to repay this kindness is by producing good results.

Next, I would like to talk about my experiences of golf in the United States. It was a positive experience to be able to play in the States, where the environment is different to that of Japan, and to play with people from different countries.

My impression of the States had been that the people would be in good shape and able to hit the ball very far. However, as far as I saw, none of the Americans we played were hitting the ball much further than anyone else. What I mean by this is that I realized I could keep up with my American counterparts. I don't mean that we were close, I mean that I think that I might be capable of beating them. Having said that, I wasn't able to record great results in the States, so I still have a long way to go. I thought I wasn't any good. But I have to use this as a springboard, and learn how to get stronger.

Haruki Miura

iii. What should we leave behind?

Sometimes, when people inherit assets, they rely on those assets, using them as a platform upon which to live their lives. But those same people can start to neglect new fields, new ideas, new research. Since there is no need for them to struggle, to work. In the world of business, it is not unusual for the second generation, which has inherited the business, to squander everything the parent has built up. We need to be hungry.

The focus of Ohshiro's interest is shifting steadily onto people. I have already discussed his interest in the elderly. Caring for the elderly is a topic of national importance. And I have talked above about his interest in young people. Ohshiro wants to see young people grow into global men and women, able to stand alongside and talk to people from the rest of the world as equals. This isn't limited to sport; he wants to see young people success in business, in international politics. The future is in the hands of the young people of Okinawa and of Japan. We need to care for them, provide them with resources, and introduce them to the world.

Money will eventually run out if you use it all, but spending money on the young is an investment in the future. While it is of course acceptable to leave assets behind, investing in the next generation is true corporate social responsibility. Enagic, now a globalized company, has been supported by many countries across the world and has profited from that support through revenue. Giving back to the local community is the best way to express gratitude. As the Romans said, "Money is like drinking saltwater, the more you drink, the thirstier you get".

b. Inward flowing currents

Today, Enagic is pushing for greater development through globalization. This is not progress without strategy. Here I would like to introduce some of the plans in place to help achieve that.

i. "Let's Unify 20,000"

This slogan exemplifies a short-term objective for the company; to reach a monthly sales total of 20,000 units. It is a means to realize a strategic approach for the States, the EU, Asia, and new markets.

This rallying cry is testament to the fact that while Enagic has focused, up until now, primarily on the American market, the company is now taking a more global perspective. The States is the launch pad from which the company has expanded into other countries, but the combined scope of the remaining markets— still to be developed—is huge. The pace of growth in the Asian market has been rapid, overtaking that of the States, and the market is still young; it is overflowing with "vibe". The "vibe" that resonates throughout Hong Kong is the same across the Asian market. When it comes to staff, too, it seems likely that we will stop thinking about staff as being appointed to the "American" or "European" or "Asian" branches of the business; instead, we will have one "global" staff.

In this way, "Let's Unify 20,000" is more than just a simple sales target. It has a wider meaning; it is a call to bring the whole of Enagic together, to enable the ideas and the impetus of the staff to transcend regional borders and differences and instead take on a global scope. It is also an opportunity to bring about greater efficiency through the integration of operations. This is a time to think about the entire company united together, with esprit de corps.

Alexander the Great, King of the Ancient Greece kingdom of Macedon, decided that it was his mission to bring together east and west. He then used his military might to achieve his goal. Will the globalizing Enagic Group, under its slogan of "Let's Unify", be able to achieve the same thing?

ii. Global strategizing in the palm of a hand

The term "global village" is a relatively new expression. It expresses the notion that richer countries will help to support poorer countries, but it is also a product of today's age of high-tech communication. The rapid acceleration of the pace of communication has meant that even those "villages" which are, geographically speaking, located far away from each other are now, in terms of the speed of communication, no further apart than two neighboring villages. The speed is almost instantaneous. The transition from postal mail to e-mail has led us to an age of impatient communication; nobody can wait. If you receive an email yet do not reply within a few hours, the sender will think you slow to reply. Having to wait until the following day for a reply inevitably creates an impression of "lateness". This is the time we are in now.

The emergence of smart phones has further compounded this need for speed. Of course they enable quick communication and are multi-functioning besides, making them extremely useful. You can send and receive mail wherever you are. You can work quickly, whenever and wherever, making your response more efficient. A standard smart phone is small enough to fit into a shirt pocket, or in the palm of your hand; it takes just a single finger to operate. High-tech applications such as this will doubtless have a significant role to play in Enagic's strategy for globalization. While the systems needed for globalization might be ready to go, in terms of the inherently complex process of practical application, we need to refine those aspects which are still incomplete. The team responsible for systems development at Enagic notes the following benefits of high-tech applications:

- New business development possible in the palm of your hand
- Able to place product orders regardless of time zone or location
- Fast handling of business inquiries, recruitment, revenue
- A selection of languages available, scope of business activity widens
- Registration and product ordering become paperless systems

iii. Global training by the Professional Development Department

The Professional Development Department was established in early 2014. Katsumasa Isobe, a veteran of forty years, was put in charge. The basics of training are not, in fact, what we would call sales know-how, in other words what to sell and how to sell it. Instead, this is high-level training, touching upon such topics as renowned psychologist Abraham Maslow's theories of motivation and self-expression, and Freud's theories on human nature. Isobe informs me how the book they use in training, *Setting Off towards a New You*, covers everything from Freud's theories of human nature through to the theory of "transactional analysis" (TA), developed by American psychoanalyst Eric Berne. It has been used widely in education and training in corporations and organizations.

I have attended one of Isobe's seminars; it was rich in information, so much so that we almost forgot to have lunch. The seminar was held in a hotel in Los Angeles, in December of 2014; around eighty people took part in the four-day training course. On the evening of the final day, certificates of completion were handed out before the training was brought to an end with a closing dinner.

Several people had travelled significant distances to attend: there were six people from Indonesia, for example, as well as a few from the EU and the East coast of the States. Attendees need to be of a

certain rank of distributor to attend training. After the presentation of certificates, some of the trainees stood at the podium to speak about their experiences and to give further encouragement. "We are all one", said one of the trainees. "We are all connected by love", he continued. "We are the Enagic family, we will achieve our objectives". He did not speak in terms of business; his comments were focused on the idea of the trainees as a fellowship with the Enagic fellowship. It was a clear outcome of the TA training he had just received.

This sort of training is just the sort of fresh air needed to breathe new life into Enagic's endeavors to move from the American market into the EU, Asia, and new markets beyond. As we come closer to having one million distributors on board, a shared belief among those distributors of themselves as a fellowship, as the Enagic family, will be crucial in linking the distributors together to generate a significant synergistic effect. The Professional Development Department has a major role to play in Enagic's globalization.

iv. Kangen turmeric supplements

Okinawa has a long history of turmeric cultivation. Back when Okinawa was known as the Ryukyu Kingdom, there was considerable trade between the islands and mainland China. One of the main exports to China was turmeric. Put simply, turmeric was a goldmine for the islands. Turmeric is a popular ingredient in the spice powders used to make Indian curries, and so of course is grown in India. The rich variety of spices found growing in India made the country a prime target for European nations. It is likely that China imported turmeric from the Ryukyu Kingdom because of its high quality. Today, Enagic is in the process of repeating that history, by developing a global business based on turmeric exports. One of our staff has dubbed this "Ukonomics" after the Japanese term for turmeric, *ukon*.

Okinawa has the perfect environmental conditions and climate for growing turmeric. How well the plant grows and its quality is determined by the weather and the soil. In particular, the mountainous Yanbaru region to the north of the main island is ideal for growing turmeric. Conditions are so good that American researchers specializing in turmeric have visited the island to conduct fieldwork. Enagic's *kangen* turmeric is made using turmeric grown in the Yanbaru region. The company signs contracts with local farmers for the supply of turmeric, and oversees production. Unlike most of the turmeric available on the market, Kangen Ukon™ is grown organically; no chemical fertilizers are used at any stage in the production process.

The Yanbaru region has soil so rich that it is termed the "jewel of nature" by local people. High quality turmeric grows here, blessed by just the right number of hours of the warm Okinawan sun at just the right angle. Kangen Ukon™ is available in soft jelly capsules, which contain, alongside turmeric, such antioxidant-rich ingredients as pure olive oil, *shiso* (Perilla herb), flaxseed oil, and *kombu* (kelp) extract.

The main weapon in Enagic's artillery is the *kangen* water machine, but Ohshiro has been pursuing research, investigation, and development into kangen turmeric for a decade. The result is the Kangen Ukon™ supplement. Full-scale sales of the supplement in the States started in April 2013. The approach to marketing the product is unique; commission for sales of Kangen Ukon™ is "piggy-backed" onto that for sales of kangen water machines. It is a system designed to encourage business growth. For the distributors, it's a way of killing two birds with one stone. The plan is to extend the market for Kangen Ukon™ from the States into Europe and Asia as well as new markets.

Enagic Kangen Ukon™ has also been awarded a patent from the government of Japan for the process behind the creation of each capsule.

v. Strategic expansion: a second factory in Okinawa

Certain parts of Okinawa are designated as special economic zones; the costs of setting up a business in such a zone are alleviated in part by such measures as leases and tax benefits. Establishing new businesses and expanding existing businesses inevitably involve risk, and the upfront investment required includes a significant amount of initial capital. Special economic zones focus on these issues and try to create strategically attractive packages for business owners.

This is where Ohshiro's latest dream lies. His eyes are drawn to a point far beyond the ocean horizon, past any (undecided) future factory site. As he stands on the site, planning the construction of his next factory, what is it that Ohshiro is really thinking?

There are a number of advantages in building a second factory in Okinawa. For a start, the factory would be closer, geographically, to continental Asia than the Osaka factory, and, as we have already established, the Asian market continues to show huge potential for growth. Having the site of production close to the markets on which products will be place results in significant advantages. The need to respond to the globalization of markets is of utmost urgency. Locating a factory site within an area that offers preferential measures can mean considerable savings. Of particular relevance is the fact that the cost of labor is cheaper in Okinawa than it is in Osaka or Tokyo. The fixed costs associated with a factory are also lower. The construction of a second factory will doubtless result in major contributions to the growth of Enagic both in Japan and internationally; it is certainly something to look forward to.

Constructing a second factory is an idea that comes from forward thinking, toward the next generation of Enagic. It is Ohshiro's hope that his eldest son, Hiroki, will take over the family business. A second factory would give Hiroki a platform from which to launch his career.

Hiroki does not resemble his father; he is unusually tall considering the height of his parents. He is a pleasant young man, a good person. As his father edges ever onwards, like a stealth samurai, Hiroki is close behind, quietly following his father's lead. His current inconspicuous presence tells us that right now he is undergoing the training he needs to run the company in the future.

vi. Research into US medical approval for kangen water

In 2012, Enagic USA became the only company in the industry to be awarded with special certification from the Water Quality Association (WQA), a status that has significantly enhanced the reputation of the company. At present, Enagic is pursuing research through a third-party research company in order to obtain medical certification from the Federal Drug

Administration (FDA) and the Environment Protection Agency (EPA). According to Dr. Horst Filtzer, the medical advisor for Enagic USA, the FDA will award medical device status to products beneficial to human health. For example, pacemakers have been awarded medical device status for their ability to prevent death resulting from abnormal cardiac rhythm—an obvious beneficial effect. If Enagic can show, through medically robust evidence, that its products can have a similarly beneficial effect, then it should be possible to obtain medical device status from the FDA. To obtain this status, Enagic must demonstrate, using medical data, how the antioxidant intake can have a beneficial impact on health. To do this, we are focusing our efforts on empirical tests to demonstrate antioxidant activity in red blood cells. Dr. Filtzer has been using Enagic products at his own clinic for many years and is well aware of their benefits. He is looking forward to seeing the results from Enagic's continued testing. If the results are as expected, Dr. Filtzer believes it will be possible for Enagic to receive approval from the EPA as a hard surface disinfectant for both commercial and household settings. This would then pave the way for an application to the FDA.

There is much to look forward to in the future for Enagic products. Incidentally, Dr. Filtzer graduated from the highly distinguished Harvard Medical

School and specializes in vascular medicine. After graduation, he served as a medical doctor in the US Army, during which time he was deployed to Vietnam during the Vietnam War. On his return, he worked at Boston City Hospital, military hospitals, and private hospitals, before taking up his current position as Director of the Wound Care Center in Western Arizona Regional Medical Center, Bullhead City, AZ. His resume includes a glowing recommendation of kangen water, as a "great benefit to all mankind".

vii. Enagic experiments with Wagyu beef

Ohshiro's only son, Hiroki, guided me to a spot in the centre of the grounds of the Enagic Country Club. We had arrived at a cattle shed. Here, amazingly, the club was raising Wagyu (Japanese) cattle, giving them only kangen water to drink. In yet another unique idea, Ohshiro was trying to develop "Enagic Wagyu" cattle. The plan was to have the cattle drink only kangen water, thereby raising them to be unique to Okinawa—a new breed of Wagyu, the Enagic breed. A young employee—a member of the Enagic Baseball Team and a graduate of an agricultural high school— was responsible for looking after the five adult cattle and one calf. All were the offspring of the same adult. I asked the young man a few questions, if only to alleviate my half-suspicion that Ohshiro was just playing around.

The process of raising cattle for consumption involves rearing calves and farming the cattle for beef. Enagic concentrates on rearing, raising the cattle on kangen water and observing and documenting the results. Okinawa cattle are renowned for the quality of the beef, which—like the famous Okinawan kurobuta breed of pig—is extremely delicious.

Cattle breeders on the mainland of Japan take calves from Okinawa and raise them into Kobe cattle and Matsuzaka cattle—two of the best known brands of Wagyu beef in Japan. This was the first time I had heard this fact, and it made me realize that perhaps, in fact, it would not be too long before we saw Enagic beef from Okinawa on our dinner tables.

I decided to ask Ohshiro directly. I asked him where the idea for Enagic beef had come from. His reply was straightforward: "One of our staff members was a graduate of an agricultural high school, so it would have been a waste not to use his experience, and anyway he seemed very keen". I could only murmur in agreement at the simplicity of the reasoning.

Enagic's main business is selling kangen water machines. That main business is going well so what possible reason might there be to get involved in cattle breeding, a field which bears no relation whatsoever to the main business? But if I think about it a little harder, things become clearer: neither people nor animals can survive without water. And it goes without saying that the water they take into their bodies will have an impact on their health. That being the case, it seems only natural to feed *kangen* water to cattle. It's not just a question of the quality of the beef; it's an interesting experiment in terms of the benefits and impact of *kangen* water.

We often hear stories of Enagic distributors who only give their pets kangen water to drink. It's not unusual to hear about pet owners who treat their pets as if they were children, only giving them bottled water. The pet market is growing year on year, with sectors expanding to include medical care, insurance, hotels, funerals, and cemeteries. The world is certainly a strange place.

2. The World of Network Marketing

Around the time when network marketing was introduced to Japan, there were hopes that this new approach to business would lead to a revolution in product distribution. In Japan, distribution channels are complex; there are multiple layers, which means that there is considerable time and cost involved in getting a product from the producer to the end consumer. Business was crying out for a distribution revolution. However, network marketing has sparked controversy in Japan. It is seen in the same way as pyramid schemes or confidence tricks. This widely held misconception is one of the reasons for the lack of understanding among people in the industry and the lack of application of this approach to business in Japan. The Japanese government should be looking to remove the irresponsible restrictions put in place by the Act on Prevention of Pyramid Sales, as well as protect and nurture network marketing, and incubate the industry under government direction. In the States, network marketing is a huge industry; it has been accepted and naturalized. Globally, network marketing is growing annually and there is much for Japan to learn from this phenomenon.

a. The global market for network marketing

According to data from the World Federation of Direct Selling Association (WFDSA), there are around 91,500,000 salespeople involved in networking marketing businesses worldwide. These salespeople are motivated by a variety of reasons: the opportunity to work part-time, financial independence, boosting income, learning new skills, self respect, of the desire to give something back to the local community. Data for the same year indicates that worldwide revenue was $153,700,000,000. We can compare this to the annual budget for the whole of Okinawa prefecture; in 2013, that was $7,190,338,500. So global sales are approximately twenty times that of the Okinawan prefectural budget, with American sales alone making up a total over four times that of the budget.

Revenue in the States currently stands at around $30,000,000,000 dollars. This is an increase of $10,000,000,000 from a decade ago. Japan has the second highest annual sales total in the world, at $24,000,000,000, which is still significantly higher than China, the third-ranked country. Looking at performance by sales, the rest of the top ten countries in 2010 were as follows: Brazil, South Korea, Mexico, Germany, Russia, Italy, France. Incidentally, Enagic Global has a presence in the following countries, the global rankings of which are indicated in brackets: Canada (11), Malaysia (12), Taiwan (13), Thailand (14), United Kingdom (15), Australia (17).

There are 22 countries in the world with total revenue sales of more than one billion dollars. These 22 countries represent 90% of network marketing sales worldwide, while the top five countries account for 60% of global sales. Statistically, while sales in certain countries might be flat, sales in developing Asian economies are showing continued growth. In those countries where sales are flat, the number of networkers is still increasing.

In 2011, in those countries where sales are rising are showing increases of 18%. If we consider that 85% of the world's population lives in these countries, as well as this rate of increase, it seems clear that these countries have enormous potential for market expansion. The desire of the people in these countries to improve their living standards can surely contribute to this market expansion.

In terms of global trends, most networkers are women, at around 75%. This trend is particularly strong in Latin American countries, where 90% of marketers are women. In Enagic, we must use this sort of statistical data to develop effective marketing strategies.

According to the United Nations, the global population is aging rapidly; it predicts that by 2050, 60% of the Asian population will be elderly. In anticipation of this, a certain network marketing business has predicted an annual 20% rise in anti-aging products over the next few years. This prediction hints at what could be a significant market for Enagic Global, too. As living standards improve and people accumulate more material wealth, this will lead to an increase in the amount of money people are prepared to spend on health maintenance, wellness, and anti-aging.

b. The MLM market in the United States

Most of the network marketing (also known as multi-level marketing, MLM) businesses in Japan are foreign-owned, with most being American: Tupperware, Shaklee, Mary Kay, Avon, Amway, Nu Skin, Herbalife. The United States is the birthplace and home of network marketing. The industry has a long history there. In the 1970s, there were a number of incidents in which the federal government tried to prosecute network marketing businesses for running pyramid schemes. Today, however, network marketing has been accepted and is employing increasing numbers of people, as we have already seen. The figures above are a clear indication of how widespread networking marketing is in the States today.

In this section, I would like to give a brief overview of the history of network marketing in the States. I will be referring to *Network Marketing: What you should know*, written by Jeffry Babener, a renowned industry lawyer and a personal friend. His book was published in Portland, Oregon, in 2001. The information below has been used with his permission.

The data used in the book is a few years old now, but it is still useful in understanding the overall flow and trends in the network marketing industry in the States. A comparison of the figures in Babener's book and those introduced here in the previous section may also provide some useful hints. The industry made a significant leap forward in a single bound as a result of globalization in the 1990s and 2000s.

A) The American market: At the time, annual global sales stood at around $80,000,000,000, half that of the current total. In other words, global sales have doubled in the decade to 2011. For the United States alone, sales have increased by $20,000,000,000, or 35%, and the rate of increase in the rest of the world is significantly higher than that of the States. It is also an indication of the globalization of the network marketing industry. It seems likely that this trend will continue.

B) Contributing to increased employment: it is estimated that, globally, every week sees around 150,000 people become newly involved in the industry, with that total standing at 55,000 per week in the States alone. Annually, 2,860,000 new networkers are born. Of course, some of these people leave the industry after a short time, while some only ever make a single sale. The current total for the States is estimated to stand at around 17,000,000. Incidentally, if we assume the current average household income to be $50,000, then the network marketing industry creates full time employment for 400,000 people. 65% of networkers are women, with the remaining

35% men. This ratio has an impact on network marketing companies and regionality. Around 80% of all networkers are part-time, with the remaining 20% working full time.

C) Networker income: the annual income of networkers is as follows:

$ 35,000 +	3.0%
$ 50,000 +	2.0%
$ 150,000 +	0.1%

These figures are from ten years ago, so today, given the market expansion and increased market competition in place, it is evident that greater proportions of marketers will be hitting these figures.

Networker ages: the average age of networkers is as follows:

25 - 44 years old	44%
45 - 54 years old	14%
65 years and above	5%

Incidentally, 8% of all networkers have some form of physical disability. This shows how physical disability is no obstacle to becoming a networker. It is also clear from the figures above that the majority of networkers are in the prime of their lives.

D) Japan is the world's biggest market: today, the American market has overtaken that of Japan, but ten years ago, Japan was the biggest market in the world. This may well have been partly because of the strength of the yen. Japan is an inward-looking country and people are extremely conscious of their status as members of a group. For this reason, Japan is often said to have the ideal conditions for network marketing: the tendencies for agreement, cooperation, and mutual assistance within the group are greater than in other countries. Markets grow through personal connections: family, relatives, friends, colleagues, and friends from home.

c. Triumph over a competitor's lawsuit

The United States is a paradise of litigation; it is a country overflowing with lawyers. I have heard that, recently, the number of people looking to become lawyers is falling, and I think that is something to be welcomed. The following anecdote comes from a friend who is a lawyer working in the automotive market: "it is more efficient to export American lawyers to Japan than to try and change the import regulations for Japanese cars into the United States". Some of the demands and assertions of rights made in the States, under the banner of the protection of human rights, work only to distort society. "We can sue whomever we want, whenever we want, for whatever reason we want". This senseless sense of legitimacy has only served to create more lawyers than needed in the country. These lawyers then encourage corporations and individuals alike to "stand up for their rights or lose out". Individuals do it and so corporations do it too, accusing competitors and dragging them into litigation. Litigation issues arise regularly within companies, too. In reality, many of these cases are conducted on a no-win, no-fee basis. As a result, the litigation never stops. Some are so far-fetched they are hard to believe.

Enagic USA has also been caught up in this sort of litigation; it took four years for the case to be over. The litigation results in huge expenses, significant internal labor costs, travel outside of the state, drawing up tens of thousands of pages of documentation, meeting after meeting with lawyers, and countless wasted days in court. It resulted in considerable losses for the company. The jury refused all ten-plus points on the complaint filed by the other company, totally absolving Enagic in a clear victory for the company.

The legal system in the States means that if someone files a complaint against you, the only choice you have is to stand up and face it. If someone files a complaint against you through a lawyer, then you have to get your own lawyer involved in order to fight the case. If you don't, you will lose even if you have done nothing wrong. The United States is a wonderful country, and many people around the world have a great love for the States. However, this misuse and misappropriation of rights is different. The fact that Ohshiro dislikes lawyers is because of the preposterousness involved in this rule of law. Discussion is always the best way to resolve conflict.

d. MLM still not at home in Japan

Why hasn't the network marketing industry yet been fully accepted in Japan? It is a welcome presence in the States, entirely accepted by society. But there remains a level of certain distrust in Japan, which the industry finds extremely difficult to shake off.

The first network marketing business launched into Japan in the 1960s; it was Tupperware, the American company. Since then, many individuals and companies have expanded into the country. In the 1990s, large MLM companies, including Herbalife and Nu Skin, entered the Japanese market. That same market continues to expand to this day.

However, other businesses also rode the MLM boom: scams and pyramid schemes. The damage caused by these sorts of schemes continues to be significant. It has caused harm to the positive image of any number of MLM companies, which otherwise work hard to make social and economic contributions, and continues to skew the reputation of the MLM industry. Put simply, pyramid schemes are not about selling products; they are about collecting membership fees from people who have been recruited into the organization. These membership fees form the basis of the profit structure of the company.

In the United States, membership fees are extremely low and are carefully regulated. As such, it is not possible to establish a business without having a tangible product, nor is it possible to increase member numbers only in order to increase revenue from membership fees. Such schemes are nothing more than malicious business practice, which expand across networks despite the lack of an actual product. It is the role of a business to provide a product or service and to receive a certain fee in return for that product or service. Without this structure, a business is not a business. Legislation has been implemented in Japan with a view to preventing scams such as these, but unfortunately they continue to be perpetuated. There needs to be a strict clamp-down on such practices if the MLM industry is to be able to grow and expand in the future.

e. The cost to Enagic Japan

Since around 2000, Enagic Japan has recorded rapid growth, opening up a number of branches across

Japan, and developing a number of new products. Several years later, the company had built up enough of a power base to start advancing overseas, gaining further force in the process. At the same time, the Enagic brand name became increasingly recognized in Japan. The MLM industry expanded into new global markets, as well as increasing the size of its market in Japan. The growth of Enagic was also the result of the market environment. As an MLM business grows, the number of distributors must also increase. Key to increasing distributors is the management of those distributors. If the company fails to adequately manage distributors, then the company will be subject to punitive measures enforced by the law. Distributors do not have the status of company employees; however, there is a regulatory requirement to see them as being under the management of the company. As such, if a distributor tells lies in order to sell an Enagic product, ultimately the company is responsible for that lie. The recruitment of distributors, sales activities, and PR must also all be carried out under the management of the company. For these reasons, the company must spend large sums on distributor training.

A company managing tens of thousands of distributors has to take on considerable administrative responsibility. There is no issue with having contact with leader-ranking distributors, but it can be extremely difficult to manage end distributors, who have never even been seen by the company. The only option for the company is to rely on the upline. New distributors begin sales activities in the field without having undergone proper training. They probably make mistakes. They might be too aggressive, too focused on getting a result on the same day, too eager to say things that shouldn't be said. Sometimes, distributors who have bought a product call the company to complain: "things aren't what I expected". This was a trend experienced a few years ago; some even called the government-run Consumer Affairs Bureau. This resulted in the name "Enagic" being brought to the attention of the authorities. The result was that the company was ordered to temporarily some of its activities. The Consumer Affairs Bureau conducted two unannounced inspections of the Tokyo headquarters, but nothing untoward was found and the company was absolved from any wrongdoing. The only problem that needed to be resolved was the strengthening of the management structure to train and manage distributors.

f. The challenge of global management

Enagic started in Okinawa, a tiny island in a single corner of Japan, but today has grown into a global company. A company that previously functioned on a single culture and a single ethnic group has thrown itself into a multi-cultural, multi-ethnic business environment. Only a dozen years have passed since the company took those first steps.

If the culture of the market is different, then the way that products are sold within that culture must be different, too. The company must build up knowledge and awareness of the culture and legal systems of the markets in which it trying to establish itself. There may be religious requirements, too. In Malaysia, for example, a prayer room must be available in one corner of the office. To the company, strictly speaking, it is superfluous space. In Japan or the United States, where there is total religious freedom, it is hard to imagine such requirements being put in place. Tax systems, business law, differences in monetary value; it is difficult to manage all these aspects adequately by relying on the knowledge of individuals alone. In product design, too, adaptations must be made for different languages; this will not work if the company insists on sticking slavishly to the same method.

The climate can also have a significant impact on business. Distributors working in Alaska, near to the North Pole, and distributors working in Cape Town in South Africa will likely be very different in their business methods and their concept of money. The top managers in Enagic, as a globalized company, need to have considerable knowledge, experience, and awareness of international etiquette. This is a pressing matter. Managers need to be able to hold their own in a global context.

Ohshiro's retirement is still a long way off. For the next ten or twenty years, his main responsibility as the owner of Enagic is to foster successors who can take over the company once he does retire. Going forward, all top managers at Enagic will need to have the following three skills sets: first, they must have strong communication skills including proficiency in English. Enagic's main market is the United States and the company is moving into the EU, Russia, South America, and of course the rapidly growing markets in Asia. Working in global cities requires English language competence. The ability to communicate in English is also necessary as a way to create contact points between Enagic staff and Enagic distributors. Staff must have effective leadership and communication skills if they are to be successful leaders. Second, they must have an international perspective. Managers working globally must have a global outlook and global ideas. Managers whose ideas are rooted only in Japanese culture and customs are not suited to today's corporate environment, in which companies must be part of what is called a global village. Third, they must have the ability to adapt to change by adopting multiple perspectives. Top managers must be able to respond to change from both inside and out, to have the capacity to adapt, to be resilient. The complex human factors involved in a multi-cultural and multi-lingual company are reflected in the markets in which the company is active; the EU market is different from the Asian market, which includes Japan. It is not enough to develop a single marketing strategy. Managers need to be able to respond to markets from multiple perspectives. Regulations issued by governments, industry, and religions can also have significant impact on markets.

It is clear that Ohshiro must maintain his command for the foreseeable future, but he also has an important task in fostering a successor. Perhaps he already has someone in mind, but whatever the case it will be extremely difficult to find someone ready and willing to step into Ohshiro's shoes.

"Dreams aren't for dreaming, they are for making come true". Ohshiro is firm in stating this belief. From his tiny island, he made his way to Tokyo, then Los Angeles, to New York, Hong Kong, and continental Asia, then onwards further to the EU: London, Paris, Germany. Now, his sights are set on Russia. He has already established a base in South America, a market with huge potential.

"Quenching the thirst for global success". Ohshiro's path to success has taken him from a tiny island to the world, yet it is no exaggeration to say that without failure and difficulty he would never have found that path. The same success that Ohshiro has found can also be found by whoever is reading this book. It is just as Ohshiro always says:

"Yes, I've done it, so you can too!"

Enagic Global Group

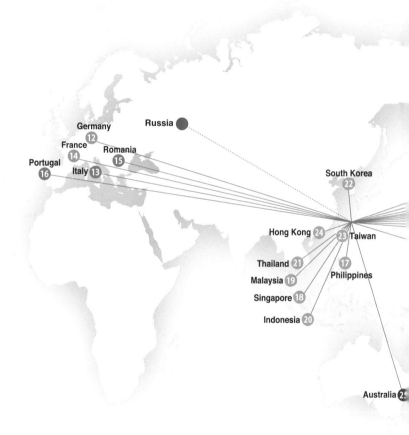

Germany ⑫

Russia ●

France ⑭
Romania ⑮

Portugal
⑯
Italy ⑬

South Korea
㉒

Hong Kong ㉔
㉓ Taiwan

Thailand ㉑
⑰
Malaysia ⑲
Philippines

Singapore ⑱

Indonesia ⑳

Australia ㉕

8 Vancouver
2 Seattle
Toronto
9
5 New York
Los Angeles
4 Chicago
1
3 Texas
6 Florida
7 Hawaii
Mexico
10

Brazil
11

■ North America
U.S.A.

❶ Los Angeles
4115 Spencer Street
Torrance, CA 90503 USA
TEL: (310) 542-7700 FAX: (310) 542-1700

❷ Seattle
19009 33rd Avenue, W., Suite 201
Lynnwood, WA 98036 USA
TEL: (425) 640-2222 FAX: (425) 672-8946

❸ Texas
739 Justin Road
Rockwall, TX 75087 USA
TEL: (972) 722-7499 FAX: (972) 722-7402

❹ Chicago
1154 S. Elmhurst Rd.
Mount Prospect, IL 60056 USA
TEL: (847) 437-8200 FAX: (847) 437-8201

❺ New York
36-36 33rd St.
4thFloor Suite 403
Astoria, NY 11106 USA
TEL: (718) 784-2110 FAX: (718) 784-2103

❻ Florida
8803 Futures Drive, Unit 01
Orlando, FL 32819 USA
TEL: (407) 601-5963 FAX: (407) 730-3335

❼ Hawaii
Ala Moana Pacific Center, Suite 711
1585 Kapiolani Boulevard
Honolulu, Hawaii 96814 USA
TEL: (808) 949-5300 FAX: (808) 949-5336

Canada

❽ Vancouver
Van City Building Suite 678
5900 No.3 Road Richmond
British Columbia, V6X 3P7, Canada
TEL: (604) 214-0065 FAX: (604) 214-0067

❾ Toronto,
75 Watline Avenue, Suite 138
Mississauga, ON L4Z 3E5, Canada
TEL: (905) 507-1200 FAX: (905) 507-1233

■ South America

❿ Mexico
Av Vasconcelos 345
col Santa Engracia
San Pedro Garza Garcia
Nuevo Leon, Mexico
TEL: +52 (81) 8242-5500 FAX: +52 (81) 8242-5549

⓫ Brazil
Rua Joao Dos Sanos,532
Jardim Santa Rosalia, Sorocaba,
Sao Paulo,18090-040 Brazil
TEL: +55-15-3033-4131 FAX: +55-15-3034-410

■ Europe

⑫ Germany
Immermannstr. 33
40210 Düsseldorf, Germany
TEL: +49 211-936570-00 FAX: +49 211-936570-27

⑬ Italy
Via roccaporena 40-42
00191 Roma
TEL: +39 06 3330670 FAX: +39 06 33213189

⑭ France
24 rue du Banquier 75013
Paris France
TEL: +33 (0) 1 47 07 55 65 FAX: +33 (0) 1 83 71 17 06

⑮ Romania
Branduselor nr: 68-70 6Th floor 500397
Brasov Romania
TEL.+40-371350042
Email:Romania@enagiceu.com

⑯ Portugal
Avenida da França, 735
4250-214 Porto Portugal
TEL.22-9698430 FAX.22-9698435

■ Asia

⑰ Philippines
21st Floor Oledan Square 6788
Ayala Avenue, Makati City, Philippines
TEL: 632-519-5508 FAX: 632-519-1923

⑱ Singapore
111 N Bridge Rd,
25-04 Peninsula Plaza, Singapore 179098
TEL: (+65) 6720-7501 FAX: (+65) 6720-7505

⑲ Malaysia
Unit 29-7, The Boulevard
Mid Valley City, Lingkaran Syed Putra
59200 Kuala Lumpur, Malaysia
TEL: 603-2282 2332 FAX: 603-2282 2335

⑳ Indonesia
The Plaza Office Tower, Lt.22
Jl. M.H. Thamrin Kav.28-30
10350 Jakarta Indonesia
TEL: +62 21 29923111 FAX: +62 21 29928111

㉑ Thailand
14th Floor, Unit 1408-1410, Park Ventures Ecoplex
57 Wireless Road, Kwang Lumpini
Khet Patumwan, Bangkok 10330
TEL: +662-116-3046-50 FAX: +662-116-3044

㉒ South Korea
7F 118-3, Nonhyun-dong
Gangnam-gu Seoul, Korea
TEL: 02-546-8120 FAX: 02-546-8127

㉓ Taiwan
Nanjing East Road, 3-337 12F B Room
Xiong Shan Qu, Taipei City, Taiwan
TEL: 886-2-2713-2936 FAX: 886-2-2713-2938

㉔ Hong Kong
Unit 1615-17, 16th Floor Miramar Tower
132 Nathan Rd., Tsim Sha Tsui
Kowloon, Hong Kong
TEL: (852) 2154-0077 FAX: (852) 2154-0027

㉕ Australia
15/33 Waterloo Rd, Macquarie Park
New South Wales 2113, Australia
TEL: +61-2-9878-1100 FAX: +61-2-9878-1200

Expanding into the New Markets

Afterword

As I put my pen down and look over my work, I realized I am faced with a rather boldly written manuscript. Some of the events I talk about in this book have been fleshed out with rich detail provided by Enagic. I was able to access data about the history of Enagic via the 40th Anniversary Commemorative Issue of the Enagic Company Magazine. I also made reference to kangen turmeric and the Enagic Training Department via translated documentation made available from the company.

I would like to thank Jeffrey Babener, a legal advisor for looking over the book.

Finally, I would like to express my gratitude to Hironari Ohshiro himself. He gave me freedom to write this book without any demands or requests with regard to content, allowing me to write freely and without restraint.

Toshio Maehara

Toshio Maehara: Profile

Born in Miyakojima, Okinawa in 1941
Graduated from Naha Commercial High School
Graduated from Okinawa University Junior College
	(night course), where he was in receipt of a scholarship
Graduated with marketing from the University of Hawaii
	on a Galileo (Fulbright) scholarship
Graduated with a MBA from the University of Southern
	California Graduate School
Graduated with a MA from the Fuller Theological Seminary
Established Maehara & Associates in 1975
Established the Gospel Venture International Church in 1994
Currently serves as pastor at the same church, and as works
	as consultant to Japanese companies
Former Member, Institute of Management Consultants,
	New York